Alexander Crowcher Schomberg

Historical and Political Remarks upon the Tariff of the Commercial Treaty with Preliminary Observations

Alexander Crowcher Schomberg

Historical and Political Remarks upon the Tariff of the Commercial Treaty with Preliminary Observations

ISBN/EAN: 9783337078195

Printed in Europe, USA, Canada, Australia, Japan

Cover: Foto ©Suzi / pixelio.de

More available books at **www.hansebooks.com**

HISTORICAL AND POLITICAL

REMARKS

UPON THE

TARIFF

OF THE

COMMERCIAL TREATY:

WITH

PRELIMINARY OBSERVATIONS.

LONDON:

PRINTED FOR T. CADELL, IN THE STRAND.

MDCCLXXXVII.

PRELIMINARY OBSERVATIONS.

I T is propofed in the following pages to offer fome general obfervations upon the conftruction of Treaties, and the qualifications of a Commercial Negotiator ; to point out that revolution in the trading fyftem of Europe, which was effected by an acknowledgment of the independent fovereignty of the United States of Holland, at the Treaty of Munfter, and to confider its principal variations and improvements fince that period, in a deduction of fome remarkable facts from the hiftories of France and England. Such an Inquiry, impartially conducted, may not be thought unfeafonable, at a time when the public attention is fixed on an important object fo intimately connected with it. The particular reafons for what has been attempted towards changing the form of our prefent Commercial Treaty, will hereafter be explained : in the mean while it will appear fufficient juftification to alledge, that by varying the fituation of a picture, there is fometimes a chance of bringing it into fuch a light as fhall produce a more ftriking effect, and difcover beauties and connections which had before efcaped the eye of

B   the

the obferver. It is hoped, moreover, that this Inquiry will not upon the whole be found lefs interefting or fatisfactory, if, preferring the inveftigation of truth to the gratification of party; it prefent itfelf, at firft, under a form feldom adopted in popular treatifes.

MAN may be confidered as acting both in a natural and in a focial capacity. There are certain rights and obligations peculiar to each, of a quality immutable and indifpenfable. The proper confideration of thefe, marks out the diftinction between the Law of Nature and the Law of Nations; and, at the fame time, teaches us, why, though different in their application, they muft in their origin be the fame. That which in one cafe is faid to be the law of nature, regulating the conduct of individual men, is in the other, only the fame law applied to the direction of individual communities. States, thus contemplated, affume the perfonal properties of men, and may acquire rights, and contract obligations, by exprefs engagements. Hence arifes what has been termed, the Conventional Law of nations; which, though capable of being varioufly modified, and adapted to the exigences and characters of particular states, yet springing, as we have seen, from the same pure source, the law of nature muft be admitted, like that primary law itfelf, to bind the faith of focieties in public treaties and negotiations.*

. Since, then, all thofe rights, which ftates derive from the neceffary or natural law of nations, become, when thus qualified, the objects of pofitive convention, the conftruction of fuch folemn contracts muft furely be a work of great difficulty, and importance; requiring, in the negotiator, a fingular combination of fpeculative and experimental fagacity, and, in the contracting parties, a decided love of natural equity, and an inviolable attachment to national faith. Public Treaties, and the perfons of Ambaffadors, have accordingly been held facred in all ages and nations; though, as communities are ever actuated by the fame paffions, and governed by the fame principles, as the individuals which compofe them, we fhould not wonder to find them often expofed to corruptions and abufes. Many writers have em-

---

* PUFFENDORF. *Law of Nature and Nations,* B. II. chap. iii. § 23.

VATTEL. Pref. to *The Law of Nations.*

ployed

ployed themfelves in tracing thefe corruptions to their fource, in pointing out their fatal
confequences, in urging arguments for the
neceffity of national honour, and in illuftrating
the duties of fecial magiftracy. But, in their
reafonings on this fubject, they feem to have
overlooked a point of no fmall importance :
for, perhaps, it is the remote caufe of all thofe
corruptions which we lament. We know, that
in private contracts, precifion and perfpicuity
are indifpenfable ; yet, what is the cafe with
refpect to national conventions, which, as they
involve the interefts and happinefs of kingdoms,
cannot, either in their arrangement, or their
language, be too clear and unequivocal? We
are told of an Italian Politician, who ufed to
boaft, that he never fpoke on critical conjunctures, but in fo equivocal a manner, that his
words would bear a double conftruction : this
pernicious fophiftry, often unintentionally perhaps, has been fuffered too much to prevail in
the fcience of negotiation, and has rendered
the ftyle of fome public treaties fo embarraffed
and obfcure, and their form fo perplexed, and
void of defign, that it is very difficult to dif-
cover their meaning. It has been made an objection to fuch inftruments, that they abound

in

[5]

in needlefs repetitions, and circuitous phrafes; but, in the inftance before us, let us confider the folemnity of the compact, and the fatal confequences of its infringement, and we fhall allow, that no precaution, which can give new force to the condition, or fhut up an avenue to fubterfuge, ought to be deemed fuperfluous. The fault in fact feems to be, that their language is in general too defultory, carrying the affectation of order without its diftinctions, and abounding in terms vague and indecifive. The reafon is clearly this : Inftead of confulting the fpirit of the age in which they live, or the character and habits of the ftates with whom they treat, many negotiators have been content to copy the forms and phrafes of their predeceffors; which, however apt in their original application, muft now neceffarily be often ufed without either meaning or effect *. It is no great recommendation of thefe forms, that they

* Of this we have ftriking proofs, whenever any extraordinary occafion has rendered it abfolutely neceffary for negotiators to leave the beaten track. Compare, with a view to ftyle, the treaties between England and the Cherokee nations; or the kingdoms of Morocco, Tunis, and Algiers, and thofe with France, and other civilized ftates. Jenkinson's *Collection of Treaties*, Vol. I. p. 228. Vol. II. p. 302. 315. V. III. p. 15. 18.

B 3

originated,

originated, for the moſt part, in the Italian
ſchool of politics.

The diſtreſs to which the power of France
and Spain often reduced the ſtates of Italy,
during the 16th century, and their frequent
civil wars, gave riſe among them to numberleſs
evaſions, in their public negotiations; which,
had they been ſuffered to paſs away, with the
occaſions that prompted them, might now have
almoſt been looked upon as excuſable; but by
the pernicious ſedulity of ſome learned men,
they have been ſo carefully collected and arranged as to form, in a manner, a ſyſtematic
code of political chicane; abounding in principles which are as diſgraceful to national wiſdom,
as inimical to natural juſtice. Hence it hap-
pens, that the adjuſtment of theſe ſolemn compacts has ſometimes been treated as little more
than a trial of dexterity in the art of over-
reaching; where it is the intereſt of each party
to circumvent the other by fineſſe, to perplex
buſineſs by ſubtleties, and to introduce every
propoſal in dark and ambiguous language. *
When we recollect with what ſcrupulous order
the ceremonial of a congreſs for ſettling theſe
national

---

* One of their principles ſeems to have been, that treaties with infidels need not be conſidered as binding. But
(we reaſon from VATTEL) the law of nature, and not re-

national compacts, is conducted, and reflect on
the studies and habits of those persons who com-
pose it, we are naturally led to expect some ap-
pearance of *arrangement* in the result of their
deliberations. But this is not always the case.
How many treaties are there, the materials of
which seem thrown together, without any de-
sign, or even an attempt at arrangement, infomuch that it is almost impossible to form a clear
idea of what may be their object or effect, till
viewed under a new disposition; since it is not
uncommon, beside the want of order in particular articles, to find an interesting stipulation
abruptly suspended by the intervention of a
new subject, and as unexpectedly resumed in
some other part of the treaty. *

                                            These

ligion, regulates the treaties of nations, who negotiate
with each other in the quality of Men, not of Christians,
Musfulmans, &c. A religion which should teach the contrary, and allow of infidelity in such contracts, could never proceed from the Author of Nature, who is always con-
stant and faithful. (*Law of Nations*, B. II. ch. xii. § 162.)
Let it be remembered, that *Mahomet* urged to his followers,
the necessity of an inviolable observance of treaties. Ock-
ley's *Hist. of the Saracens*, V. I. p. 76.

* This want of order in arrangement is feelingly re-
gretted by a great Political Arithmetician, in the case of
public papers, laid before the House of Commons;
(Young's *Annals of Agriculture*, No. xxix. p. 396.) and

Thefe objections will receive ftrong confirma- tion in the inftance of marine treaties, in which the negotiator has certainly better opportunities of preferving fimplicity of language and arrangement, than in the more multifarious bufi- nefs of a general pacification. In no branch of diplomatics, however, have thofe principles of natural equity, which conftitute the law of nations, been more accurately defined, or more happily adopted into common practice, than in the regulations of commercial intercourfe. We muft not therefore be furprifed, if, in the mi- nuter departments of fuch negotiations, fome deficiencies fhould occur; for they require an infight into remote confequences, which nothing but long and practical experience in mercan- tile affairs can furnifh, and which, therefore, feldom falls within the reach of a ftatefman. The eftablifhment of a Committee, for the pur- pofe of preparing bufinefs of this kind for public debate, compofed of men qualified, by their education and profeffion, to form accurate opinions on fubjects of trade, and who, by an extenfive correfpondence, are accuftomed to inveftigate the caufes, and forefee the effects,

it muft be obvious to every perfon, who has had occafion to confult a collection of treaties, or any other documents, with a view to accurate information.

of

of every variation in the commercial balance,
it can never be doubted would remove all defects of this kind, and is recommended by the
example of the greateft trading republic of
modern times. A committee of the Privy
Council can never be adequate to fuch an
undertaking in its full extent, for the fame
reafons which difable many negotiators; and
the judgments of individual merchants is objectionable; becaufe, however qualified in
other refpects to give advice, they muft of neceffity clafh in their interefts and prejudices, fo
as to make it difficult to draw as clear a deci-
fion from among them, as would be the refult of
an experienced committee. Without fome fuch
plan as this, it is furely unreafonable to expect
that perfection in marine treaties, which their
importance requires; becaufe, however brilliant
in the higher branches of his office, a negotiator is very rarely qualified for the profeffional
labour of detail and calculation.* This appears

on

* Though I entirely agree with Mr. Young in his
idea of the mifchievous effects of the *monopolizing* fpirit, I
cannot fubfcribe to his opinion that this evil can be increafed by fuch an eftablifhment as a *Chamber of Commerce.*
" Annals of Agriculture," Vol. III. p. 452. On the contrary I am at prefent perfuaded it muft, among other advantages, contribute much to counteract it. In this I am
poffibly miftaken, and fincerely wifh that he would take an

on the flighteft view of the department; but, were we to confider it more fcrupuloufly, it would be found to demand fuch a variety and extent of talents, as few minds are capable of difplaying. Befide a general knowledge of the trade, and reciprocal interefts, of the contracting powers, he ought to be precifely acquainted with their feveral kinds of induftry and fkill; to dif-cover their wants, to calculate their refources, and to weigh with nicety the ftate of their fi-nances, and the proportionate intereft of their money; nay, further, he fhould be able to afcer-tain the comparative population and ftrength of each country, together with the price and qua-lity, both of firft materials, and alfo of the labour beftowed upon them; for this purpofe he fhould inquire into the operations of every clafs of merchants and manufacturers con-cerned in the treaty, fhould confult their ex-pectations on each of its feveral branches, and collect their hopes and fears on the effect of fuch a commercial revolution, on the competition of rival nations. A good treaty of commerce, in-dependent of the art of negotiation, is pro-

early occafion to enter more fully into this important fub-ject, for which, by his long experience and acute genius in fuch matters, he is fo eminently qualified.

nounced

nounced by one, who well knew the extent and
difficulty of the fubject, to be " a mafterpiece
of fkill." *

The ABBE DE MABLY is of opinion, that
particular regulations in commercial treaties are
contrary to the true intereft of ftates. Were
this doctrine once eftablifhed, the bufinefs might
be comprifed in a very narrow compafs, and all
this detail of qualifications rendered uneffential
in the character of a plenipotentiary. After
certain general rules for the freedom of commerce and navigation are adjufted, he thinks it
would be more prudent for each party to truft
for the reft, to their internal policy, and to
enact, among themfelves, fuch laws as may be
calculated to promote domeftic induftry, and to
enable their own fubjects to furpafs their neighbours in all the great articles of traffic : " For,"
he adds, " every advantage granted to foreign
trade is, in fome degree, a check upon your
own. It creates a competition ; and, what was
at firft a particular privilege, becomes a general
right : in the mean time, that branch of your
domeftic trade, whatever it be, inftead of receiving an extenfive circulation from the unre-
ftrained induftry of the people, is thus confined

POSTLETHWAYTE's *Commercial Intereft of Great Britain,* V. II. p. 423.

by

by foreign competition, and, in the end, entirely ftagnates."* But fuch a fcheme as this feems objectionable on many accounts. It is at prefent only neceffary to obferve, that its adoption would defeat the leading idea of marine compacts, which are intended, not merely to lay down general rules for the freedom of commerce and navigation. Thefe are now fufficiently underftood, and practifed by every civilized power, being founded on certain immutable principles, which have one only criterion of juftice ; but rather to reconcile the interefts of the contracting parties, in many particular branches of trade ; which, depending, in a great degree, on the variable tafte, manners, and ingenuity of mankind, muft for ever ftand in need of periodical revifions. That fuch are the leading objects in modern conventions, will appear more fully from the following reflections.

THE TREATY OF MUNSTER, among other vifible effects on the law of nations, produced a confiderable revolution in the commercial policy of Europe. When, by this Treaty, the United States of Holland obtained the acknowledgment of their fovereignty, they vigoroufly applied themfelves to thofe arts, by which alone they had been enabled to maintain

* *Droit Publique de l'Europe*, Tom II. p. 561.

the

the conteſt; and to ſecure, at laſt, their freedom and independence. Ambition, not avarice, is uſually the characteriſtic vice of nations;
but, whatever tranſient influence ambition may
have had on the oppoſers of Spaniſh tyranny,
during the ſtruggle, it was a paſſion by no
means calculated to take root and thrive in the
conſtitution of a Dutch republic. What had
coſt them ſo much unabated labour to obtain,
they reſolved to preſerve by a uniform ſyſtem of
ſhrewd, ſelf-intereſted policy.* That commerce, which had been gradually increaſing for
more than half a century, it was now their firſt
care to extend and confirm by cautious negotiations.

The inactivity of thoſe maritime ſtates, which
had always conſidered traffic as an object of too
little dignity to be made the foundation of national grandeur, afforded them the opportunity;
accordingly in leſs than fifteen years from the
Treaty of *Munſter*, there was ſcarcely a power
of any conſequence with whom they had not
formed an advantageous alliance, merely with
a view to commercial privileges. The perfection
to which they carried the trade of *freightage*,

* See *The Political Maxims* of JOHN DE WITT, a work
which proves its author to have been equally calculated to
ſhine in the Compting-houſe and the Cabinet.

was a stroke of policy peculiar to themselves; and to this they were firſt led as much, probably, by their ſituation as their avarice. Among many other new regulations for its ſupport, they appear to have introduced thoſe laws for adjuſting neutral traffic with belligerent ſtates, which now make ſo marked an article in all treaties of navigation and commerce;* the laws alſo of contraband were greatly improved by them, and the various ſpecies of mercantile property more accurately defined and ſecured.†

The

---

* The *Hanſe Towns* were the predeceſſors of the Dutch in the Carrying-Trade, but never enjoyed it ſo excluſively, or in a manner ſo effectually ſecured to them. It ſeems as if the article, alluded to above, was firſt admitted by France, in a treaty of defenſive alliance between her and Holland, in 1662; and, being renewed in the Marine Treaty of 1678, has been ſince continued, and repeatedly confirmed. As this Treaty of 1662 was taken as the baſis of that commercial compact, which followed the Triple Alliance in 1668, it was admitted alſo at that time by the Engliſh, and repeated in the treaty of 1674, which now regulates, for the moſt part, our trade with Holland. Jenkinson's *Diſcourſe on the Conduct of Great Britain to Neutral Nations,* p. 30.—*Collection of Treaties,* V. I. p. 190. 202. 211.

† The regulations of contraband are founded on very rational principles, long in uſe among maritime ſtates. In the " Conſolato del Mare," a code of high antiquity, we read:----"in hoſtium eſt partibus qui ad bellum neceſſaria hoſti adminiſtrat." tit. 276. But there are many diſtinc-

The science of negotiation became thus enriched
with clearer maxims of maritime jurifprudence,
and almost a new title added to the code of the
law of nations.

There are marine treaties between many
European ftates, to be found in the hiftory of
very early ages; though they chiefly-confift of
combinations for mutual defence against pirates,
whofe depredations in the Mediterranean and
Baltic obftructed the commercial intercourfe of
thofe times, and rendered alliances of this fort
very neceflary; yet this was not, as fome have
afferted, their only object. The utmoft extent
of their views, however, feems to have com-
prehended little more than provifions for certain tolls and duties, and general engagements
for the protection of the perfons and property of

tions neceflary to modify this rule. See MOLLOY *De Jure
Maritimo et Navali*, B. I. c. i. § 12. et feq. The fourth
article in the treaty of 1674, already mentioned, was fuggefted by Queen Elizabeth's remarkable capture of the
Hanfeatic fhips, bound to Lifbon, with corn, for the fupply of the Spaniards. It has been uniformly held, that
goods calculated merely for luxury or pleafure, can never
be ranked as contraband. Upon this principle, in the
year 1676, when the French and Dutch were at war, the
Englifh permitted the French to build a pleafure yacht for
their King at Portfmouth, and it was not confidered as a
breach of the neutrality. MOLLOY, ut fupra, §. 24.

merchants

merchants, trading to, or resident in, their respective dominions.* —Even in ages much nearer our own, we have frequent instances of the contracted scale of their negotiations. There is indeed, a Treaty between England and France, in the year 1514, which comprises some articles of reciprocal advantage in many useful branches. But this is, I believe, almost the only exception.† Even the Society of the Hanse Towns, a confederacy, both in its object and importance, unrivalled in ancient or modern history, though known to have made considerable progress in commercial policy, as far as regards municipal institutions, yet, if we except some cautious stipulations, for privileges and protection in the ports of England and Denmark, never appears to have engaged very deeply, or to have adopted any system in its negotiations with foreign powers.§ Whoever shall compare the maritime conventions of earlier ages with "the particular article concerning navigation "and commerce," inserted in the Treaty of

* RYMER's *Fœdera*, Tom. V. p. 740. 763.

† Ibid. Tom. XIII. p. 412.

§ WERDENHAGEN, *De Rebus publicis Hanseaticis*, Tom. I. p. 73. and *the Convention at Lubec*, in 1613, Tom. II. p. 140.

Munster

Munfter, the fubfequent Treaty between Holland and England, or England's Treaty with Portugal in 1654, by which fhe acquired a free trade to the Portuguefe Colonies in Eaft India, will be convinced that the Treaty of Munfter is the æra whence we ought to date our prefent fyftem of naval and mercantile policy.* Till that period, the outline was faint and contracted; it has fince gradually acquired boldnefs and extent. In fhort, it was referved for the fuperior fagacity of modern nations, founded on the experience of paft ages, and for thofe more humane virtues, which now characterize and adorn fociety; to introduce an enlarged fpirit of hofpitality into our marine conventions, which has given an expanfion and ftability to trade beyond all former examples; which has opened an unreferved communication between almoft every region of the habitable earth, and nearly fwept away all ancient prejudices, arifing from diftinction of language, manners, or government. This fpirit has lately diffufed its influence over the rude inhabitants of the Baltic coafts,‡ and feems at laft about to complete

its

* JENKINSON's *Collection of Treaties*, V. I. p. 42, 45, 72.

‡ *Treaty of Commerce and Navigation between Great Britain and Ruffia, in* 1766. JENKINSON's *Treaties*, V. III. p.

its work, by marking out the ground for a reconciliation between two great kingdoms, whose hereditary enmity has too often disturbed the tranquillity of Europe.* From these necessary reflections, we are now naturally led to the immediate subject of our present inquiry, and to some other matters, connected with it.

224.—*Treaty of Commerce between Russia and Denmark, in* 1782, V. III. p. 268.—*Between Russia and Portugal, in* 1783, V. III. p. 314; and, in the same year, *An Edict of the Empress for a Free Trade,* V. III. p. 331.

* "Commerce," says the Author of *The Spirit of Laws,* "is a cure for the most destructive prejudices; and to this "it is we are in a great measure indebted for the present "polish of European manners; because, having diffused a "general knowledge of the manners of all nations, there "naturally arises a comparison between them, and hence "results the advantage." *Esprit de Loix,* Liv. XX. ch. i.

Treaties are the Statute Laws of a statesman. Considering their importance, it is surprising that we have no collection of them sufficiently complete. RYMER brings them down to the year 1642; from that period, THURLOE's *State Papers* may be usefully consulted. *A General Collection of Treaties,* in 4 vols. 8vo. published in 1732, and JENKINSON's *Collection of Treaties,* in 3 vols. 8vo. concludes them at the late Peace in 1783. A well arranged code of public treaties, with such historical and political remarks as should not only illustrate every material article in them, but also should compare and connect their partial and general effects, would surely be a valuable acquisition to the diplomatic science.

THE

THE TREATY OF NAVIGATION AND COM-
MERCE between France and Great Britain,
figned at Verfailles the 26th of September
1786, confifts of 47 articles. Having premifed,
according to ufual form, that there fhall fubfift
a reciprocal and perfect liberty of navigation
and commerce, between the fubjects of the two
contracting parties, for all kinds of goods in
their refpective dominions in Europe,* it proceeds, in the firft place, to extend certain privileges and protections to the perfons and property of merchants refident in either country,
and permits them, even in cafe of a rupture
between the two crowns, to remain, and continue their trades, without any interruption;
but in cafe their conduct fhall render them fuf-
pected, the term of twelve months is allowed
them to remove, with their families, property,
and effects.† Befides free permiffion to vifit,
dwell in, and pafs through each other's dominions without paffports, the fubjects of both
kingdoms have licence reciprocally to import
in their own fhips all merchandizes and goods,
not prohibited by law, into the dominions of
either party, to refide therein, and to buy and
fell lawful merchandizes there, in any manner
whatever; nor are they, on this account, to be

---

* Art. 1.　　† Art. 2.

　　　　　liable

liable to any duty or imposition, except such as shall be afterwards specified, or to which the inhabitants of the country are liable;* it is therefore thought reasonable ‡ to abolish the Capitation Tax, and the *Argent du Chef*, and to prohibit the future introduction of any such arbitrary impost.‡ Freight duty, likewise, on ships belonging to his Britannic Majesty, is removed, and, in return, the duty of five shillings is taken off French ships.† Disputes in the ports of either kingdom, between the commander of a ship and his seamen, are to be settled, for the present, by the magistrate of the place; requiring the person accused to give the accuser a written declaration, witnessed by

* Art. 4, 5. The laws of England have ever been favourable to merchants. By *Magna Charta* the effects of foreign merchants are protected against seizure or confiscation, in case of war. Cap. xxx. Upon which MONTESQUIEU observes, how high an idea one must entertain of the spirit of a nation, where such a clause is made an article of its liberty! *Esprit desLoix*, Liv. XX. ch. xiii.

‡ Art. 12. In countries where the ease, comfort, and security of the inferior ranks of people are little attended to, *Capitation Taxes* are very common; because, being levied at little expence, and rigorously exacted, they afford a very sure revenue to the state. SMITH's *Wealth of Nations*. B. V. chap. ii. V. III, p. 330, Edit. 1786.

† Art. 15.

the

the magiſtrate, whereby he ſhall be bound to
anſwer that matter in his own country, and after
this it ſhall not be lawful for the ſeamen to de-
ſert or detain the ſhip. For the ſtill further
encouragement of foreign merchants in both
countries, among other ſmaller privileges, they
are permitted to keep their accompts, and to
hold correſpondence, in what language they
pleaſe, nor, unleſs in caſe of bankruptcy, are
their books, or other inſtruments of trade, liable
to be ſeized or inſpected.＊ They are moreover
left entirely free to tranſact their own affairs, or
to employ whom ever they ſhall think fit; as alſo
to load and unload their ſhips, without interruption or interference of any Port-Officer whatever.‖
To complete the catalogue of theſe immunities,
they are permitted the free exerciſe of religion,
and the rights of ſepulture in the dominions of
either ſovereign.‡ Theſe articles, thus ſelected
and claſſed, ſeem properly to fall under one
head, and may form the firſt diviſion of the
Treaty.

＊ Art. 17.　　　　‖ Art. 18.

‡ Art. 5, latter part. Moſt of theſe immunities have
been partially introduced into all commercial Treaties,
even as far back as the middle of the laſt century. See
Treaty of Commerce between England and Portugal in 1654.
Art. XIV. and *between England and France, in* 1655. Art.
XII.

　　　　　　　The

The TARIFF declaring the duties apportioned to feveral forts of goods and merchandizes by this compact, the mode of levying them, and fome Cuftom-Houfe regulations, may be fo connected as to form a fecond divifion, though ftrictly confidered, the fixth article alone contains the tariff of the treaty. Of this article, therefore, it is unneceffary here to fpeak, for an obvious reafon. I fhall proceed to the other parts of this fecond divifion. After fpecifying the rates on the moft effential objects of commerce, and agreeing not to alter them, but by mutual confent, it is ftipulated, that all other merchandizes whatever, belonging to the fubjects of the two fovereigns, fhall be admitted into their refpective dominions on the footing of the moft favoured European nation, and that fuch fubjects themfelves fhall be included in all additional advantages, which may hereafter be on either fide extended to navigation and commerce. * So likewife, in cafe either of the contracting parties fhall eftablifh prohibitions, or fhall augment the duties upon any part of the growth or manufacture of the other's country, not fpecified in the tariff, thefe fhall be extended generally to the fame goods and mer-

* Art. 7.

chandizes

chandizes of the moſt favoured European nation; and, if it ſhall revoke prohibitions, or
diminiſh duties, on the growth and manufactures of any other European nation, the ſame
advantages ſhall be granted to the other contracting party, on condition of reciprocity. *
In all this, however, there is a reſervation † to
France in favour of Spain, agreeable to the
24th Article of the Family Compact of 1761,
and to England, in conſequence of her Convention with Portugal in 1703. No pretence
of any fraud or defect whatever, ſhall hereafter
impower any perſon to inſpect or confiſcate the
exportations of either country, but the buyer
and ſeller are perfectly free to adjuſt their own
price and bargain. ‡ Neither ſhall ſhips or cargoes be ſubject to confiſcation, on account of
any manifeſtly unintentional miſtake or error in
their entry or declaration; nor merchants, or
maſters of ſhips, be liable to any penalties on
this ſcore, if the goods omitted ſhall not have
been landed prior to the declaration. § And

---

* Art. 11.

† Art. 7. and 11. For the particulars of theſe reſerva-
tions ſee *The Family Compact in* JENKINSON's Treaties,
Vol. III. p. 70; and *The Treaty of Commerce between England and Portugal*, Vol. I. p. 353.

‡ Art 8.　　§ Art. 10.

　　　　　　　further,

further, to prevent impofitions and frauds,
fuch merchandizes as are contained in cafks,
chefts, and other cafes, fhall henceforth only
pay duty for their real weight *.

The third head, under which the Treaty
may be diftributed, is, by much, the moft extenfive, comprifing many very material points
of maritime jurifprudence. In the 'firft place,
in order to regulate the doctrine of contraband
in time of war, by clear and exact principles,
we have, in feparate articles, two large cata-
logues of fuch goods as do or do not fall under that defcription; † the refult of which is,
that all arms, military implements, and fol-
diers on their voyage to employment in a military capacity, in either the fleets or armies of
an enemy, fhall be deemed contraband; as
alfo money and provifions which are in the
act of conveyance to any place of an enemy,
befieged, blocked-up, or invefted, and as fuch
they may be feized and confifcated; in all
other cafes, the fhips and merchants of either
contracting party have full liberty to fail to the
ports belonging to the enemies of the other
party; and to pafs, not only between fuch ports
and neutral places, but alfo from one port of

* Art. 9.   † Art. 22, 23.

the

the enemy to another, and therein to traffic, without oppofition or difturbance ; and the like immunities are extended to the perfons and property of enemies found on board the fhips of either of the two contracting parties. But, on the other hand, the perfons or property of either of the contracting parties, found on board enemies fhips, though not falling under the title of contraband, are not to enjoy the fame privilege, it being a fettled maxim, that free fhips make free cargoes, and the contrary.* For the effectual prevention of difputes and mifunderftandings, in thefe matters, it is further agreed, that in cafe either party fhall be engaged in war, the fhips of the other party fhall be furnifhed with paffports, drawn up according to a form annexed to the treaty ; and alfo with certificates, fpecifying the feveral particulars of the cargo, the place whence the fhip failed, and whither fhe is bound ; and fuch fhip, falling in with the men of war or privateers of the other party, having exhibited her paffport and certificate

---

* Art. 20. 29. Much ufeful information and found reafoning on this fubject may be found in JENKINSON's *Difcourfe on the conduct of Great Britain with refpect to neutral nations,* prefixed to his *Collection of Treaties* ; and in MOLLOY, *De Jure Maritimo et Navali,* B. I. ch. iii. §. 9. and the following.

(to

(to which the master is compellable), shall have liberty to proceed on her voyage without search, chase, or any molestation whatever.*
But if a merchant ship be not provided with such passports and certificates, yet, upon examination before a proper judge, and upon sufficient proof of her belonging to the subjects of either party, she be found to contain no contraband goods, she may be released, together with her cargo, in order to proceed on her voyage. † It is also provided, that even in case of a discovery of contraband goods, it shall not be lawful to proceed to any act whatever of breaking open, or removing the same, till the lading shall be brought on shore, in the presence of proper officers, and an inventory made by them of the said goods. Neither shall it be lawful to make any use or advantage of them till after sentence of confiscation, pronounced upon them, in due and lawful process, before the Judges of the Admiralty; the ship itself, and the other goods therein, being entirely free from confiscation or detention on account of the prohibited goods, agreeable to a stipulation in a former article. ‡

* Art. 24. 26, 27.   † Art. 33.

‡ Art. 20. 28.

To

To thefe provifions for the free and honourable maintenance of commerce, in times when
either of the parties fhall be engaged in hoftilities, and for the prevention of fraud and fubterfuge, which are the never failing fources of
difcontent and animofity, it is further agreed,
that no acts of hoftility or violence fhall be
exercifed by the fubjects, &c. of either of the
two crowns againft the fubjects of the other on
any pretence whatever; neither fhall they receive
for fuch purpofe a commiffion or patent of any
kind, from any prince or ftate, at enmity with
either party, to act or arm as privateers or letters of reprifal, againft them, under the fevereft
punifhment, befide being liable to make full
reftitution and fatisfaction to thofe whom they
have injured. Nor fhall either of the contracting parties grant letters of reprifal againft the
other, unlefs in the cafe of an injury, after proper application made to the minifter refident in
the injured country, no redrefs can be obtained,
and juftice is obftinately denied or delayed. †

Nor

---

† *Reprifals*, by the laws of England, are of two forts,
ordinary, and *extraordinary*. The ordinary are either
within the realm or without. Thofe within the realm are
granted by the Lord Chancellor, by Writ of Chancery,

with

Nor shall any privateers, bearing commissions of a state at enmity with either party, be suffered to arm in the ports of the other party, to carry on any traffic there, or even to purchase more provisions than may enable them to reach the nearest port of that inimical state : moreover, no shelter or refuge shall be given to such as have made prize of any ship or vessel belonging to either party ; nor shall the ships or goods of one party be suffered to be taken within cannon-shot of the coast, or in the ports, &c. of the other * On the

---

with the approbation of the King or Council, to arrest the merchant stranger's goods here in England, of that nation which hath committed the injury. Those granted in the *ordinary* way, to repair injuries out of the realm, are always under the Great Seal, and are confidered as irrevocable, and as creating and vesting, as it were, a national debt in the grantee, to be satisfied, as is directed in the patent, out of the goods of that nation whence the injury proceeds. *Extraordinary Reprisals* are called *Letters of Marque*, and are granted by the Secretaries of State, with the approbation of King and Council. They are during the King's pleasure; and, being intended only to harass or weaken the enemy in war, are always revocable. MOLLOY, B. I. ch. ii. FITZHERBERT, Nat. Brev. fol. 114. Stat. 4. Hen. V. c. vii. xiv.—Ed. IV. c. iv. et 4 Inst. 124, 125. 137.

* Art. 3. 16. 40. latter part 41. It has been deemed a violation of the law of nations to assault an enemy in the

the contrary, their majesties' ships of war, or the privateers belonging to their subjects, may carry the ships and goods, taken from their enemies, whither they please; neither shall any prize of this kind, brought by them into their respective ports, be liable to inquiry, search, detainer, or seizure. * Ships of either of the two nations, retaken by the men of war or privateers of the other, if they have not been in the power of the enemy twenty-four hours, shall be restored to the owners, upon their paying a stated sum, specified in the article, for their redemption. † And in all disputes respecting the legality of prizes, the judge shall direct an inventory and an appraisement to be made of the effects, and shall require securities from the captor, for paying the costs, and from the claimant, for paying the value of

port, or under the protection, whether of friend, ally, or neuter. See a very remarkable case of Sir KENELM DIGBY, with the French, Venetians, and the Grand Seignor. MOLLOY, B. I. ch. iii. §. 7.

* Art. 40, first part.

† Article 34. HALL's *History of Pleas of the Crown*, p, 163. *Consulatu Maris*, cap. 283. 287 : but in general this law of *Restitution* is extended, in all possible cases, in favour of the owner. MOLLOY, *De Jure Maritimo et Navali*, B. I. ch. ii. §. 21.

the

the prize on either iffue of the fuit; and in fuch
cafe of proper fecurities given, the execution
of the Judge's fentence fhall not be fuf-
pended by reafon of any appeal. * 'Ships or
merchants of either kingdom, fuffering any
injury or outrage from the men of war or privateers of the other, fhall have ample repara-
tion; to which intent the perfons and effects of
the offending party, fhall ftand bound; but in
the cafe of any kind of torture ufed by a captor
upon the mafter, crew, or paffengers, not only
the captured fhip itfelf, together with the perfons, merchandizes, and goods, fhall be forth-
with releafed, but alfo fuch as fhall be convicted of the crime, together with their accom-
plices, fhall fuffer the moft fevere punifhment.
With this view, all commanders of privateers,
before they receive their commiffion, &c. fhall be
obliged to give fufficient fecurity, by good bail,
as fpecified in the article, that they will make
complete fatisfaction for all injuries or damages
which may, during the cruize, be committed by
themfelves, their officers, or others in their
fervice. † The fhips of either party driven by
ftorm

* Art. 36.

† Art. 30. 42. 31. Thefe articles, originally inferted
in the Treaty between France and England in 1677, are,
fays MOLLOY, for their excellency, fit to be a ftandard to
all

ſtorm! into any port of the other, ſhall not be compelled to unlade, or pay any duty; and in caſe, having firſt obtained lawful permiſſion, they unlade, and ſell a part of their cargo, for the purpoſe of victualling or refitting, they ſhall only pay duty for that part. And when entered into port, in any manner whatever, they are unwilling to land their cargoes, or break bulk, they ſhall not be obliged to give an account of their lading, unleſs ſuſpected, on ſure evidence, of carrying prohibited goods to the enemies of either of the two contracting powers. In caſes of ſhipwreck, all that ſhall he ſaved muſt be reſtored upon claim made, to the proprietors or their factors, paying only the expences of the preſervation, according to the eſtabliſhed rates of ſalvage. *

After all theſe mutual agreements, with reſpect to their conduct towards each other, the contracting parties think it for the ſtill greater ſecurity of trade and navigation, to combine againſt the common enemy of commercial intercourſe; it is accordingly determined not to admit, harbour, protect, or aſſiſt in any port, city, town, or dwelling whatever, any Pirates,

all the nations of Europe. *De Jure Maritimo et Navali*, B. I. ch. iii. §. 8, 9.

* Art. 19. 25. 37.

or

or Sea-Rovers, and that perfons convicted in fo
doing fhall fuffer condign punifhment; moreover, that all the fhips and cargoes, taken by pirates, and brought into the ports of either kingdom, fhall be feized, and the property, being
fufficiently proved in the Court of Admiralty,
fhall be delivered to the owners or their factors,
even though it has paffed into other hands by
fale, if it be proved that the buyers knew, or
might have known, that they had been piratically taken. And fimilar cautions fhall be ufed
with all fhips and merchandizes taken on the
high feas, and brought into the ports of either
nation. * Such is the fum of the various materials

* Art. 39. This Law of *Reftitution* to the owner of his
property, piratically taken, is founded on Stat. 27 Ed. III.
c. xiii. and is in the true fpirit of the famous ATINIAN
LAW, *De Ufucapione*, which provided, that *prefcription*
fhould not avail againft goods fraudulently taken. "Quod
furreptum eft, ejus rei æterna auctoritas efto." But common law bars the claim of the owner, if his goods have been
fold in market overt. AULUS GELLIUS, Lib. XVII. c. vii.
ROLLE's *Abridg.* 520. YELVERTON, 135. 1. SIDERFIN,
320. 367. By 28 Hen. VIII. c. xv.—11 and 12 W. III.
c. vii.---4 Geo. I. ch. xi. §. 7, all pirates fhall be tried
as felons, and fhall be excluded their clergy. Moreover,
piracy and robbery on the feas is excepted out of the
general pardon of felonies, both at common and ftatute
law, for it is a fpecial offence, and therefore fhould be
efpecially

rials felected out of the Treaty, which appear more immediately intended to promote the freedom and fecurity of commerce and navigation ; and to them may properly be fubjoined the following articles, without which the wifeft and moft equal code would want its full effect and fanction.

In as much as it is propofed, by the prefent Treaty, in all the aforementioned refpects, the Protection of individuals,—Their Perfonal Liberty,—The Safety of Merchandize, Goods, and Effects,—The Succeffion to Perfonal Eftates,— all matters relative to the Lading and Unlading their fhips, and other privileges and immunities, that the fubjects of the two Crowns fhall, in their refpective dominions, be on the foot of the moft favoured nation; and that there fhall be an impartial adminiftration of juftice ; care is to be taken that all judgments and decrees, upon marine cafes, in the Court of Admiralty fhall

efpecially mentioned. Coke, 3 Inft. tit. Admir.--20 Geo. II. c. lii. § 13. Molloy, B. I. ch. iv. " Formerly it was " only cognizable by the Admiralty Courts, which proceed " by the rules of the civil law, but Stat. 28 Hen. VIII. c. xv. " eftablifhed a new jurifdiction for this purpofe, and fince " that time marine felonies are tried by commiffions of oyer " and terminer, under the King's Great Seal." Black- " stone's *Comment.* B. IV. ch. xix. § 5.

D   be

be given in conformity to the rules of equity,
and to the stipulations of this Treaty, by Judges
who are above all suspicion, and who have no
manner of interest in the disputed cause.* And
upon proper complaint of injustice, their Majesties shall respectively cause any sentence to be
revised and re-examined in their councils, and
shall provide that justice be done to every com-
plainant within the space of three months.
Further, in matters of dispute, the subjects of
each party may employ such advocates, nota-
ries, sollicitors, and factors, as they think fit.‡
And, lastly, for their mutual advantage, their
Majesties shall respectively appoint national Con-
suls, in the dominions of each other, to superin-
tend the interests, and to guard the privileges of
their trade.†

This

* Art. 44. 32. The original Court, to which questions
of this sort are permitted in England, is, the Court of Admiralty; and the Court of Appeal is, in effect, the King's
Privy Council, the members of which are, in consequence
of Treaties, commissioned under the Great Seal for this
purpose. 22 Geo. II. c. iii. BLACKST. Comment. B. III. ch. v.
CLERKE's Praxis Curiæ Admir.

‡ Art. 35. 38.

† Art 43. The term of this Treaty is by Art. 46, fixed
at twelve years, at the expiration of which, a twelvemonth
is to be allotted for its necessary revision. It is always
prudent.

This clofes the third and laft general divifion of the Treaty. Should there be any truth in what was before infifted upon, namely, that as diforder is a radical defect in every work of human fkill, it is particularly objectionable in matters of fo extenfive and important a nature as national compacts, then this new diftribution may not it is hoped be without its advantage; fince even the prefent treaty with all its excellencies will not perhaps be found altogether free from this common defect. If, therefore, by thus prefuming, not only to comprefs and arrange its materials, but, in fome inftances, to vary its language, I fhall be thought to have given it a more interefting and intelligible form, this merit muft at leaft be allowed me to claim, that I could not have felected from the whole diplomatic code a more honourable teftimony to the juftice of my affertion.

Among other hafty obfervations on this Treaty, it has been difcovered to be derived, through the Treaty of Utrecht, from one ratified between France and England in the year 1677. But, inftead of refting our inquiries upon a period

prudent, fays VATTEL, to limit the term of a commercial treaty; becaufe, from the nature of its object, conjunctures may arife to make it, in many points oppreffive to one of the contracting parties. *Law of Nations*, B. II. ch. ii. § 29.

which

which fo neceffarily excites unfavourable ideas of the motives for fuch a negotiation with France, it would be more candid to carry them back to a remoter age, efpecially, if in that age we can trace it to a lefs corrupted fource. The Treaty of 1677 has fmall claims to originality. With regard to its principal ftipulations, they are to be found in the commercial part of the Treaty of Munfter, the acknowledged parent of the moft effential branches of all our fubfequent negotiations;* and, more particularly, (becaufe there applied to the fame object) of a treaty between France and England in the year 1655. Which though, like the reft, it was chiefly employed on the then new and favourite topic of neutralities, and on general points of maritime jurifdiction ; yet, obvioufly having for its object the eftablifhment of a reciprocal trade between the two countries, may, in this refpect, be confidered as the genuine archetype.† Hence, therefore, our inquiries will moft properly begin.

By this Treaty it was agreed, that the fubjects of England, Ireland, and Scotland might freely

---

* Treaty of Commerce between England and Holland in 1654. *Collect. of Treaties*, V. 1. p. 42.---With Sweden---Portugal---Denmark p. 69. 71. 75. With Holland again in 1668, p. 190, and again in 1674.

† *Collect. of Treaties*, V. I. p. 82.

import into France the growth and manufactures
of their country, and, in return, should receive
as freely, the wines, woollen and silk goods of
France.* This article gave great offence to
Spain. It appears, from a memorial presented
to CROMWELL by the Spanish Ambassador,
that she was the only power of any maritime
consequence, whom he had omitted in his commercial alliances. And she urges her superior
claim to the Protector's favour, on the ground
of being the first State to acknowledge the
English Republic; while, on the contrary,
France had ever been the secret fomentor of in-
surrections there.‡ When the treaty was ratified, Spain seized upon the ships and effects of
English merchants, in all her ports, to a very
considerable amount; the consequence of which
was the declaration of a war, so ruinous to Spain,
that she never afterwards was regarded by
France as her commercial rival. Beside the
removal of such an obstacle, the same effect
was still further promoted by this Treaty; for
France, by her connection with England,
was enabled to claim a share in the carrying-
trade, till then monopolized by the Dutch, and

* Art. 5.
‡ See the Memorial in JENKINSON's *Treaties*, V. I. p. 80.

to eftablifh companies and factories of her own.*
At this period therefore, I think, we may, with
fome propriety, place the rife of her commercial
grandeur.

Commerce, fays VOLTAIRE, was born in
France as early as the reign of Francis I. but
fhe died with that King, and did not revive till
a century after.† Many fteps had been taken
during the adminiftrations both of SULLY and
RICHLIEU, to regulate and improve the trade
of that country; their good effects, however,
did not become vifible till the age of Louis XIV,
towards the middle of whofe reign, the celebrated COLBERT undertook his general reform.
This minifter began with eftablifhing manufactories of various kinds, and holding out encouragements to induftry and œconomy. The
fchemes of his predeceffors, he faw, had been
rendered abortive for want of that free circulation, which in every country is fo effential to
trade; for the different provinces, being each

* It appears, from the conclufion of this bufinefs, that
GROMWELL and MAZARINE perfectly underftood each
other. The price of the Treaty was the tradition of the
Royal Family, and their neareft friends, and their banifhment from France. *Collection of Treaties,* V. I. p. 85.

† Siècle de Louis XIV. Tom. II. p. 123.

under

under its own particular government, laid such heavy and irregular duties upon the industry of their neighbours, as greatly retarded, and, in some instances, effectually shut out all communication among them. With a view to get rid of these obstructions, COLBERT removed all export duties to the frontiers, and caused a general book of rates to be made, by which all the provinces were in future to be equally regulated. Had he acted thus prudently in other points, his system would have been unexceptionable; but, by proceeding (from a false idea of encouraging domestic manufactures) to lay heavy duties and prohibitions upon the importation of all such foreign goods as would compete with their own, he threw such a restraint upon every department of trade, as prevented the full effect of many of his beneficial intentions. " He " endeavoured," says the excellent Author of the *Inquiry into the Nature and Causes of the Wealth of Nations*, " to regulate the industry and com-
" merce of a great country, upon the same model
" as the departments of a public office; and,
" instead of allowing every man to pursue his
" own interest, his own way, upon the liberal plan
" of equality, liberty, and justice, he bestowed
" upon certain branches of industry, extraor- ·

" dinary

" dinary privileges, while he laid others under
" as extraordinary reftraints. In this, and in
" many other inftances, he fuffered himfelf,
" notwithftanding his great abilities, to be im-
" pofed upon by the fophiftry of merchants
" and manufacturers."* In the year 1662, *a
Council of Commerce* was created, at which the
King himfelf very frequently prefided, who promoted, by noble premiums, the new eftablifhments in various parts of his dominions.†
Among thefe the moft remarkable were the
woollen, filk, and gobelin manufactories. The
woollen manufactory, in the province of Languedoc,‡ by its neighbourhood to the port of
Marfeilles and to Spain, not only was able to
procure the fineft materials at a cheaper rate
than any other country, but was furnifhed alfo
with commodious inland conveyance, by means
of the great canal, and with an eafy tranfport to

---

* Book IV. ch. ii. and again B. IV. ch. ix. For a fine
delineation of a commercial fyftem, fee the *Political Tefta-
ment of Cardinal* RICHLIEU; upon which it is thought
COLBERT firft founded his idea of reform. Part II. ch.
viii. and ix.

† ANDERSON's *Hiftory of Commerce*, V. II. p. 327.

‡ A manufactory of fine broad cloths was eftablifhed
alfo at Abbeville, which to this day maintains a great degree of reputation.

Italy

Italy and the Levant, where, by underfelling the Englifh, it affailed the market in a double capacity; receiving in return for its imported induftry, raw materials for the filk manufactories, on the fame eafy terms. This feemed to threaten fatal confequences to our Turkey Company, who might be confidered as almoft in their infancy,* and, through them, to our woollen trade ; but encouragements from the Crown, and timely affiftances from Parliament, co-operating with the impolitic conduct of the French minifters, enabled them to withftand the competition. Indeed, we are told, in a petition prefented to Parliament by the Weaver's Company, on occafion of the Utrecht Treaty, that between the years 1664 and 1713, our trade with thofe countries had increafed twenty times. The caufes which contributed to the embarraffment and decline of French commerce, were oppreffive and ill-regulated Cuftoms, unjuft Monopolies, the Military Ambition of Louis XIV. and, ftill more fatal than all thefe combined, Religious Perfecution, the moft effectual check upon the

---

* This Company was erected at the beginning of the century, by King James I. and its traffic was, about fifty years after, computed to bring in an annual revenue of 300,000. ANDERSON's *Hift. Com.* V. II. p. 373.

commercial

commercial fpirit of a country. To one remarkable event of this kind muft be attributed that
total revolution in trade, which has taken place,
during this century, in Europe, I mean the
Revocation of the Edict of Nantes, in the year 1685.
In confequence of this ftep, on a moderate com-
putation, about five hundred thoufand perfons
tranfported their fkill, their induftry, and their
ftock, into England, Holland, Brandenburgh
and Switzerland, to the great depopulation of
their native country, and neceffarily to the impoverifhment of the State. To the immenfe
number of thefe refugees, who fettled in England,
we are indebted for many ufeful improvements,
and curious inventions, in our manufactories of
woollen ftuffs, filk, linen, paper, glafs, hats,
watches, cutlery, hardware, and iron. But the
amazing wealth which her extenfive commerce
had accumulated, prevented France from immediately feeling the effects of this ruinous emigration, which perhaps fhe might ftill have
recovered, but for another ftep, which excited
the jealoufy of her neighbouring rival. Too
eager to monopolize the trade of Europe, it had
long been the policy of France, as already hinted,
to aim at ruining that of England by fuch heavy
duties upon many commodities as amounted to
a total prohibition, though it would have been
much

much more for her intereſt to have encouraged that predilection for her growth and manufactures which then prevailed. In fact, while we had been giving every poſſible encouragement to their manufactories, and the produce of their ſoil, they had been gradually increaſing the duties upon all Engliſh goods.* The eyes of the country were at laſt opened, and in 1678, very contrary to the inclination of the King, an act was paſſed " to " prohibit the importation of French goods, as " highly detrimental to this kingdom." The excellent effects of this law were ſoon felt ; for, in leſs than twenty years, at the Treaty of Ryſwick, the amount of our annual exports was more than doubled :† and this notwithſtanding a very material interruption, as the prohibition

* Report of a Committee, &c. in the *Hiſtory and Defence of the late Parliament*, in 1713, p. 227 and 228. Our cloths, which in 1644 paid only a duty of 9 livres per piece, or 25 ells ⅓ Engliſh, paid in 1664, 40 livres, and in 1667 this duty was doubled. In 1699, in conſequence of the peace of Ryſwick, it was reduced to 55 livres, which was adopted in the propoſed tariff at Utrecht. See a paper called " Conſequences of a law for reducing the duties on French wines, brandy, ſilks and linen, to thoſe of other nations, with remarks on *Mercator*." No. III. A miniſterial work, at that time publiſhed by DAN. DE FOE.

† ANDERSON' *Hiſt. Com.* V. II. p. 180.

was only laid for three years; and during
the remainder of Charles the Second's reign, no
parliament had affembled; the firft act of his
fucceffor was to get it repealed; fo that, from
1685, to the Revolution, this country, fays
ANDERSON, had nearly been beggared by an
inundation of French commodities.* In 1689
there was a convention between England and
the United Provinces, for the purpofe of more
effectually checking the French trade; and in
the fame year another act was paffed to prohibit
their importations.‡ If to thefe natural effects
of national jealoufy, we add the new fources of
commerce which England had now opened,
who, no longer dependent on her neighbours,
began to fupply herfelf with wines from Italy,
Spain, and Portugal; with linen from Holland
and Silefia; with paper, ftuffs and filks, by means
of the new manufactories eftablifhed at home;
and confider alfo, that the duties had now begun
to be appropriated by Parliament to particular
ufes and exigencies of State, and could not therefore be readily removed, we fhall not be furprifed
that fuch difficulties fhould have arifen at

* ANDERSON's *Hift. Com.* V. II. p. 182. *Britifh
Merchant*, p. 319.

‡ Stat. 1 W. and M. c. xxxiv. *Collection of Treaties*,
V. I. p. 292.

Ryfwick,

Ryfwick, as to have rendered it impoffible for the plenipotentiaries to fettle any tariff between the two nations, or that fince that time mutual fufpicions and prejudices fhould have increafed thofe obftacles to a commercial communication, which it is the objeft of the prefent treaty to remove.*

While the minifter of Louis XIV. was aiming to excite a fpirit of induftry among his countrymen, and to extend their foreign trade by reftrictions and monopolies, an event took place in England which laid the foundation of our future maritime glory. This was the paffing of the famous NAVIGATION ACT, upon which, and its falutary confequences, I fhall proceed to offer a few obfervations : The firft outline of this *Great Maritime Charter,* as Sir JOSIAH CHILD calls it, † was fketched in the Long Parliament, but it was not till nine years after that it received its legal confirmation. ‡

As

---

* Negotiations at Ryfwick, V. II. Mem. xxiv. p. 464, and the following.

† Preface to his *Difcourfe of Trade,* in 1698.

‡ The original idea of this act may be found in ftat. 14 Ric. II. c. vi. repeated in 4 Hen. VII. c. x. and again, in the article of wine, in 5 Eliz. c. v. § 11. Since its promulgation in 1660, it has been conftantly receiving additions

As the strength and glory of this nation avowedly depend upon its marine, and as this can
only be refpectable in proportion to the number
of its failors and fhipping, nothing could have
been more prudently devifed than an eftablifhment for a monopoly of the trade of their own
country, for the failors and fhipping of Great
Britain, which is the leading object in this juftly
celebrated Act. Till that time the Dutch had
been the factors of Europe; and, while they
employed an immenfe quantity of men and
fhips in carrying the produce of our foreign
trade, our own marine was laid by neglected,
and our feamen (except when particular cafes
called for an exertion) were totally unoccupied.
The Navigation-Act ftruck at the root of this
evil. It excluded the Dutch from being any
longer the carriers to Great Britain, or from
importing to us the goods of any other European country, and, at the fame time, encouraged a feminary for a national marine. " It is
" not impoffible, (fays Dr. Smith) confider-

tions and revifals. By 14 Car. II. c. xi. three frefh claufes
were added; and again, by 15 Car. II. c. vii. it was
confirmed by proclamation. In 1685 it laid five fhillings
per ton on all foreign fhips employed in our coal trade,
and other regulations were added by 1 Jac. II. c. xviii.—
9 W. and M. c. xxii. and later ftatutes.

ᵀ " ing

" ing upon what inimical terms we then were
" with Holland, that fome of its regulations
" may have proceeded from national animofity,
" though they are as wife as if they had all
" been dictated by the moft deliberate wif-
" dom." *   Its wifdom however has been un-
accountably called in queftion, by fome of
thofe reftlefs fpirits, whofe glory it is, in all
ages, to cavil at the moft prudent acts of Government.   Their objections are founded on
the example of France, whofe policy it has
ever been to connect herfelf as much as poffible
with neutral nations.   This ftep, it is faid,
may at firft feem impolitic, becaufe fhe employs
fuch nations as the carriers and factors of her
trade ; but hence arifes the advantage.   In
time of hoftilities fhe is enabled to convert her
merchant fhips into private fhips of war ; and,
by leaving her trade in the hands of neutral
powers, whatever fhe lofes in Freight is thus
made up by the faving of Infurance.   But this
reafoning fhould never convince us that it can
be for the real intereft of any commercial country to encourage a fyftem of maritime neutralities, by entrufting the conveyance of her
trade to foreigners ; for, in proportion as that

* *Wealth of Nations*, Vol. II. B. IV. c. ii.

trade increafes, the pofitive and relative ftrength of a ftate muft be diminifhed in favour of her rivals. To this may be added, another radical evil in fuch a meafure : It renders the manu-factures of a country in fo great a degree fub-fervient to the humour of ftrangers, that the revenue and refources of the ftate that fells will be, in fome of their moft productive branches, totally in the power of the ftate that navigates. A nation, in fhort, which is dependent upon another for the exportation of its fuperfluities, not only gives up the regulation of its own markets, but relies on others, both for the quantity and price of foreign commodities. Herein confifts the difference between what has been called an *active* and a *paffive* trade ; the former of which diftinguifhes the mercantile fyftem of Holland, from that of all other ftates, whether ancient or modern; and it is chiefly with a view to the fuperior advantages of fuch a trade, that the beft writers on poli-tical and commercial matters, fince the publi-cation of this Act of Navigation, have agreed in their opinions of its merit. Sir JOSIAH CHILD afferts, that " without it we had not been owners of one half the fhipping nor trade, nor employed one half the feamen which we did in his time," not more than thirty years from

its

its paffing. * What opinion the Dutch entertained of it may be gathered, not only from the earneftnefs with which their plenipotentiaries at Breda contended for its repeal, † but from a confeffion of one of the ableft politicians in their Republic, who fays, " by the " politic act paffed in England, in the year " 1660, it is much to be feared that the Eng" lifh merchants will in time carry away a " great part of the Dutch trade." ‡ And afterwards, fpeaking of the comparative ftate of the two countries—" Since the prohibition of importing any goods in foreign fhips into England, except fuch as are of the growth and manufacture of the country to which thofe fhips belong, all our navigation to that kingdom is at a ftand." § DAVENANT afferts, that in the year 1688, the tonnage of our mercantile fhipping was almoft double its quantity in the year 1666, owing to the falutary operation of the Navigation-Act ; || and fo dazzled was the na

---

* *Difcourfe of Trade,* ch. iv. *concerning the Act of Navigation,* p. 1, which feems to contain a complete anfwer to moft of the objections, then and fince raifed againft it.

† *Collection of Treaties,* V. I. p. 196.

‡ DE WITT's *Intereft of Holland,* Part I. ch. xxii.

§ DE WITT, Part II. ch. viii.

|| *Political Works.* B. II. p. 29.

tion by this rapid afcenfion and increafing
fplendour of trade, that the writers of
that time conceived the commercial profperity of England to be in its zenith. * A
particular revolution, effected by the Act in
queftion, is very well remarked by the Author
of the *Wealth of Nations.* He obferves, that
" fince its eftablifhment the Colony trade has
" been continually increafing, while many
" other branches of foreign trade, efpecially
" of that to other parts of Europe, have been
" continually decaying. Our manufactures for
" foreign fale, inftead of being fuited, as be-
" fore the Act, to the neighbouring market of
" Europe, or to the more diftant one of the
" countries which lie round the Mediterranean
" fea, have, the greater part of them, been
" accommodated to the ftill more diftant one of
" the colonies, to the market in which they have
" the monopoly, rather than to that in which
" they have many competitors." † Upon this
ground, alfo, objections have been raifed, to
the expediency of continuing a law, which has
not only thus diverted a copious ftream out of
its proper channel, but has drawn it from a fure

* ANDERSON, *Hift. Com.* V. II. p. 187.
† V. II. B. IV. ch. viii.

and

and regular courfe, to one which is now become at beft very precarious. * To fay nothing of the weaknefs of the latter part of this affertion, which our increafing trade with America now fufficiently demonftrates, it may be urged againft thefe objectors, that in political queftions it is not always to be confidered only what will increafe the wealth, but what will contribute to the ftrength and grandeur of a nation. Let the Navigation-Act, then, be placed in this, its proper light, and there are few, I believe, who will be perverfe enough to deny that the naval fpirit, fo peculiar to our country, is the offfpring of that ftatute; " a ftatute (to ufe the words of an excellent judge of its effects) " which alone hath fortunately outweighed all

* Suggefted by thefe, and other principles of the fame nature, a bill was lately depending in Parliament, for laying open the trade between America and our Weft-India Iflands. The object fought was the exclufive trade of America; the effect to be produced, among many other evils, would probably have been, the eftablifhment of their marine upon the ruins of our own. On this fubject confult Lord SHEFFIELD's *Obfervations on the Commerce of the American States*, efpecially p. 158 et feq. et 295 et feq. It is a work which cannot be too ftrongly recommended to the ferious attention of every well-wifher to the manufacturei, trade, and maritime power of Great Britain.

E 2 " our

" our other follies and extravagancies. Though
" condemned by some historians, and unnoticed
" by others, it hath proved the fertile source of all
" our naval power, hath operated insensibly to
" our preservation, and been the spring from
" whence hath flowed the wealth and greatness
" of England." * Of this, therefore, as of the
allowed consequence of that spirit, which became generally diffused among the people, by
the Act of Navigation, I shall now take a sum-
mary view.

·Were we to attempt to form our opinions of
the state of England's manufactures and commerce, from the Revolution to the opening of
the present century, upon the sole authorities
of political writers at those times, it would
be a task of great difficulty. Few periods can
furnish more striking contrasts of political senti-
ment. On one side we are presented with warm
and encouraging proofs of national prosperity,
on the other, with dismal calculations of de-
creasing wealth, and forebodings of general
insolvency. We are now, by the most authentic documents, convinced that the flatter-
ing side of the picture was drawn by the cor-

* JENKINSON's *Discourse*, &c. prefixed to his Treaties,
p. xxix.

rect

rect hand of experience, while the oppofite was
nothing more than the hafty refult of defpond-
ing theory. * The war which terminated in
the Peace of Ryfwick, was certainly very oppreffive to the foreign trade of this country, and,
as Mr. .CHALMERS has ftated from the firft
authority, had depreffed it in the year 1694 to
a very low pitch, + but from that time to the
conclufion of the war, it feems gradually to
have revived. During thefe convulfions, however, domeftic traffic, and the interefts of general commerce, were daily gathering that
ftrength and elafticity which foon enabled them
to throw off their incumbent weight, and to
rife to a point unknown to any former period.
Many new manufactories were eftablifhed, and
many old ones revived; in moft of which, the
fkill of the French refugees, united with our
native induftry, now feemed to promife the
higheft perfection. The opening of a national
bank greatly promoted the circulations of capitals, and foreign fifheries afforded a new femi-

* POLEXFEN's *Difcourfe on Trade, Coin, and Paper Credit.*---DAVENANT's *Difcourfe on Trade in 1698.*

+ *An Eftimate of the comparative ftrength of Great Britain,* &c. p. 62.

nary

nary for our marine. * During the short space
of four years, from the Peace of Ryswick to
the accession of Queen Anne, the rapid improvement of our national revenue is remarkably striking. In less than four days two million sterling was subscribed, and there were persons ready to subscribe as much more. " Till
" that time," says ANDERSON, " there had ne-
" ver been so illustrious an instance of England's
" opulence. And after so expensive a war,
" what an high idea must such a circumstance
" have given foreigners of the wealth and gran-
" deur of this country!" † Yet, notwithstand-
ing this assertion, founded on documents the
most incontrovertible, namely, the Papers of
various Public Offices, and the Custom-House
Books, together with many collateral confir-
mations, there were not wanting malignant and

* Jos. GEE's *Trade and Navigation of Great Britain*, edit.
1755, p. 5. At the Revolution the value of our annual
exports was 4,086,087l. In the year 1694, in consequence
of the war, it sunk below the amount at the Restoration,
which was 2,043,043l. and, though at the peace of Ryswick in 1697, it had greatly recovered, yet it did not equal
the amount at the beginning of the war.

† *History of Commerce*, V. II, p. 223. At the peace of
Ryswick, the value of our exports was 3,525,907l. in
1701, 6,045,432l.

wrong-

wrong-headed men, who, as in the former reign, reprefented the trade of the nation to be in a precarious and expiring ftate. * " Such " proceedings," fays the elegant Eftimator of the Strength of Great Britain, "caft a juft cenfure " on the furious party contefts, during the laft " years of Queen Anne, in refpect to the con- " dition of our commerce; as if the profpe- " rity or the ruin of manufactories and trade, " were influenced by the continuance of ftatef- " men in the poffeffion or in the expectation of " emoluments and power." † The contefts here principally alluded to, are thofe which broke out in confequence of the *Propofals made in the Negotiations at Utrecht for a Commercial Treaty with France.* This event has been lately fo often alluded to by party writers, on each fide of the queftion, and is fo clofely connected with our prefent fubject, that I fhall make no apology for introducing fome particulars of it. And to this I am the more willingly led, be- caufe, among all their mafs of materials, I have not been able to collect any account of the tranfaction fufficiently difpaffionate to be

* W. WOOD's *Survey of Trade.* See particularly the vile Dedication to King George I. p. 9.

† CHALMERS's *Eftimate,* &c. p. 84.

E 4   either

either faithful or confiftent. Upon the recollec-
tion of fome circumftances which have been
ftated about the refpective fituations of France
and England, at the latter end of the laft century, their flourifhing trade, ftill in the remembrance of our people, the infant ftate of many of
our moft valuable manufactures, together with
thofe illiberal prejudices, and impolitic jealoufies,
which fettered commerce with heavy duties and
prohibitions, it will not feem furprifing that any
negotiation between the two countries on the
foot of reciprocal advantage, fhould, in the
year 1713, have been an alarming and unpopu-
lar meafure.

For the origin of the tranfaction we muft go
back to the year 1709, when the EARL OF
SUNDERLAND directed the Commiffioners of
Trade and Plantations to confider on a Treaty of
Commerce with France; and a correfpondence
was accordingly opened between fome of the firft
merchants, in each nation. Mr. ST. JOHN, afterwards LORD BOLINGBROKE, was very affiduous
in this bufinefs; and, upon the reprefenta-
tions of thefe merchants, and the written refult
of this correfpondence, he drew up a rough
draught of a marine treaty, and laid it before
the Houfe of Commons in 1711. It was by

them

them tranfmitted to a committee of merchants, and upon their opinion and revifion it was made the bafis of the Utrecht negotiation.* Many claufes are faid to have been copied from the ineffectual propofitions made at Ryfwick, and were for the moft part of a general nature ; tending to adjuft the forms and conditions of commerce and navigation, agreeable to thofe rules of univerfal equity, which the maritime States of Europe had for fome time agreed in adopting, for their mutual convenience. Had the Treaty contained nothing more than this, it would have paffed without a murmur ; but there were, unfortunately, two Articles, which feemed to ftrike at the root of our national wealth and commerce. The former of which *in general terms placed France and Great Britain in a commercial relation to each other, on the foot of the moft favoured nations* ; the latter more *particularly fpecified* the nature and extent of thofe terms ; ftipulating, among other things, *that no more cuftoms or duties be paid for goods and merchandizes brought from France to Great Britain, than what are payable for goods and merchandizes of the like nature imported into Great Britain, from any other country in Europe. That all laws made in Great*

* Journals of the Houfe of Commons, Vol. XVII. p. 347.

Britain since the year 1664, *for prohibiting the importation of any goods and merchandizes, coming from France, which are not prohibited before that time, be repealed, and that the general tariff made in France in the year* 1664, *take place there again, and the duties payable in France by the subjects of Great Britain, for goods imported and exported, be paid according to the tenor of the tariff above-mentioned, with an exception however to certain merchandizes, that is to say, manufactures of wool, sugar, salted fish, and the product of whales.** The Treaty containing these articles was signed at Utrecht on the last day of March, was ratified by the Queen, and published by Royal Authority in the month of April 1713. On the 14th of May it was moved in the House of Commons for leave to bring in "A Bill to make effectual "the 8th and 9th Articles of the Treaty," which was carried by a majority of 252 votes, against 130, and it was accordingly ordered for the 30th of the same month.‡ An order was at the same time made for an exact statement of the whole amount of imports and exports of the woollen manufacture with France, and with

* Art. 8 and 9. JENKINSON's *Collection of Treaties*, Vol. II. p. 45.

‡ Journals of the House of Commons, Vol. XVII. p. 352, and the following.

Portugal,

Portugal, from 1668 to 1669, and alfo of the wines of France and Portugal, imported into London and the Out-ports during 16 years, namely, from 1696 to 1712, to be delivered into the Houfe.* No fooner was the bill made public, than a univerfal clamour was raifed againft it by the merchants and manufacturers. Petitions, Memorials, and Remonftrances were fent from all quarters of the kingdom. The Turkey Company, the Companies of Hudfon's Bay, and of Eaft and Weft India; ‡ the cloth, filk, and woollen manufacturers took the alarm, and it at laft became fo general, that not only the principal towns and trading companies in Great Britain, but even our Factories at Hamburgh and Portugal fent their Remonftrances to Parliament. † National jealoufy had been

---

* Commons Journals, Vol. XVII. p. 365, and the following, wherein may be feen the various ftatements.

‡ Commons Journals, Vol. XVII. paffim from p. 350.

† The alarm of the Eaft-India Company arofe from that part of the 9th Article which ftipulated in favour of *goods and merchandizes of Great Britain to be imported into France.* They confidered themfelves as excluded the benefit of this claufe, unlefs the favour were extended to the produce of other countries, to be imported into France, in Englifh fhips. Their fears, however, were appeafed by a promife that fuch an amendment fhould be propofed.

2 awakened,

awakened, and the minds of the people prepared to reject any overtures for mutual advantages of trade with France, by a Bill which was brought into Parliament at the opening of that Seffion, for fufpending for two months the duty of 25l. per ton on French Wines imported, and which had produced a very fpirited Memórial from the Portuguefe Envoy, declaring, in the name of his royal mafter, that " in cafe the fubject of the 9th " article of the Treaty fhould be confirmed by " Parliament, and the Wines of France be " brought down to a level with thofe of Por- " tugal, he would immediately lay a prohibition " on all Englifh goods imported to his coun- " try."* Though of courfe each feparate petition, &c. drew its argument of complaint from the probable injury which that clafs of men, by whom it was prefented, were likely to fuffer; yet there was little variety in the general fub- ftance and tendency of the objections. It was urged, that Parliament, by paffing the Bill, would not only take the regulation of the balance of trade out of their own hands, but alfo would grant advantages to France, without an equal return; that, by her connection with

* *A Hiftory and Defence of the late Parliament*, publifhed in 1713, p. 233.

Spain,

Spain, and the superior convenience of her ports, she could procure some of the most valuable articles on much more easy terms than English traders could, and the price of labour being two thirds lower than in England, they could work up their materials cheaper, and consequently could undersell them in every market. Thus, in the first instance, they must lose the trade of Spain, Italy, and Turkey, in which their Woollens alone had brought in, for many years past, an annual revenue of 326,000l.* That, besides this loss, the trade to Portugal, to the amount of 600,000l. per ann. must fall, for it was clear that country would never consent to admit it on terms less advantageous to her than the Treaty of 1703,‡ which would be grossly violated by reducing the duties on French wines, to the same

* In *The Flying Post*, a newspaper at the beginning of this century, a writer, who signs himself—" A Dealer in " Woollens and Linens," says, " In King William's war I " sold much English woollen and linen, made in imitation " of French ; but in the late interval of peace, finding the " sale slacken, I imported French, paying the present high " duties for every piece, and sold it to so good profit, that " I totally quitted the English." No. 3402, July 18, 1713.

‡ KING, in his Dedication of *The English Merchant* to PAUL METHUEN, asserts, that the exports to Portugal, in consequence of this Treaty, were in his time from 500,000l. to 1,500,000l, per ann.

rate

rate with thofe of Portugal.* That from thefe
confiderations, and fome others which were
ftated, the manufactories of woollen and filks,
juft growing into ftrength, would be particularly
checked and diminifhed, by which an immenfe
number of hands would be thrown out of employment, and thus the landed intereft receive a
fevere blow by the fudden increafe of the poor.‡
Befide thefe complaints from the mercantile
parts of the kingdom, fcarce a day paffed without fome Pamphlet, either in oppofition to, or
in defence of, the Articles ; the principal of
thefe were *Mercator* and the *Examiner* in fupport
of the Bill, which were anfwered by the other
party in a paper called *The Britifh Merchant*, or
Commerce preferved.†

On the 30th of May, the Bill was read for
the firft time, and the 4th of June was named
for the fecond reading; it was then referred to
a Committee of the whole Houfe for amendment and revifion. Many days were employed
in infpecting the accounts given in, purfuant to

* Art. 2. *Collection of Treaties*, Vol. I. p. 353.

‡ See the different Petitions, &c. in the *Commons Journals*,
Vol. XVII.

† This laft Paper has fince been collected and publifhed
in 3 vols. 8vo.

order, from the Cuſtom-Houſe books, and in
examining merchants and manufacturers; at
laſt, on the 18th, the queſtion being put, Whether the Bill, as amended by the Committee,
ſhould be engroſſed, " A debate aroſe (ſays
" a political writer of that time) perhaps of the
" greateſt importance to this kingdom, of any
" that has happened in Parliament ſince that of
" the *Abdication*." * Among the principal
ſpeakers againſt it was General STANHOPE,
who, after much ſtrong and pointed reaſoning,
entered into a ſort of comment on the prohi-
bitory Act of Charles II. already mentioned. †
He was ſeconded by Sir PETER KING, Mr.
GOULD, Mr. HAMPDEN, and, above all, by
Sir T. HANMER, whoſe conduct in this buſineſs reflects ſuch high honour on his integrity,
that it deſerves to be particularly remembered.
Before he had heard the ſentiments of the people, moſt intereſted in its fate, he gave his vote
in favour of the Bill; but his apprehenſions for
the trade, the manufactures, and the landed intereſt of his country being now alarmed, by the
numerous and preſſing remonſtrances againſt it,

* *Hiſtory and Defence of the late Parliament*, in the year
1713, p. 243.

† Ibid. p. 43. See alſo GREY's *Debates*, Vol. V. p. 34.

he

he was not afhamed of correcting his opinion.
After a long and, very elaborate difcuffion of
the fubject, and a review of all the grand arguments, both within doors and without, which
had been urged on each fide, he concluded:—
" While I have the honour to fit in this Houfe,
" I will never be blindly led by any miniftry,
" nor be biaffed by what might weigh with
" others—the fear of lofing their elections.
" The principles on which I act are, the in-
" tereft of my country, and the conviction of
" my judgment, and on thefe two confidera-
" tions alone I am againft the Bill." * Mr.
ARTHUR MOORE, who was faid to have been
chiefly employed in conducting the Treaty,
was the leading fpeaker for the Bill. After
very warm debates, which lafted from three
o'clock in the afternoon, till eleven at night, it

* Sir T. HANMER was, in the following year, elected
Speaker of the Houfe; and, on his introduction, was com-
plimented by Sir RICHARD STEELE, in a fpeech, which
ended with thefe words.—" It is a demonftration, that the
" Bill of Commerce was a moft pernicious Bill, and no man
" can have fo great merit to this nation, at this time as he,
" by whofe weight and authority that pernicious Bill was
" thrown out. I rife up to do him honour, and, in fome
" meafure, to diftinguifh myfelf by giving my vote for
" that, his ineftimable fervice to his country." GREY's
Debates, Vol. V. p. 40.

was

was thrown out by a majority of 194 to 185.
" Thus by nine votes," fays the Hiftorian of
that Parliament, " did the trade of Great Bri-
" tain, and all its manufactures, efcape the
" moft fatal blow that ever was aimed at it." *
It may not be unamufing to know what effect
this ejectment of a Bill, which had created fuch
a ferment, produced on the commercial and
manufacturing part of the kingdom. Information of this fort cannot be had with greater
marks of certainty than from the newfpapers of
thofe times; for, till the fpirit of party was fuffered to creep in and debafe their authority,
newfpapers might be confidered as faithful chro-
nicles of popular opinion, and national manners.
" The laft poft from Somerfetfhire," fays one
of them, " brings advice, that, as foon as the
" great cloathing town of Froome had the news
" that the Bill was thrown out of the Houfe,
" the clothiers, and others, concerned in the
" woollen manufactory, made extraordinary re-
" joicings, with ringing bells, bonfires, illumi-
" nations, and drinking loyal healths to the
" Queen's Majefty, and the fucceffion of the
" illuftrious Houfe of Hanover." + In the

* *Hiftory and Defence of the late Parliament*, p. 247.
+ *Flying Poft*, No. 3392, June 25, 1713.

F   next

next number is a letter from Canterbury, which
fays—" with joy we hear, that on Thurfday laft,
" the 18th, of June, 194 Patriots did by their
" refolution fave many thoufands of poor fami-
" lies, amongft the woollen, linen, and filk
" manufactures, from utter ruin." * Such are
the accounts from the weft and eaft, which agree
exactly with what was heard on the occafion
from the central and northern parts of the kingdom. A letter from Coventry calls the ejectment of the Bill, *The glorious Negative*; and,
after much more in the fame ftrain, this poft-
fcript is added. " Great inquiries are making
" how our two members voted on this grand
" queftion ;" † a hint which fufficiently explains
Sir T. HANMER's allufion, and, which, at the
enfuing canvafs for the new Parliament, was
very generally taken. Among other inftances
of this, at the end of an advertifement for the
election of members for the county of Suffex,

---

* *Flying Poft*, No. 3393, June 27.

† No. 3394, June 30. As a fpecimen of popular wag-
gery at that time, we are told, that " a long pole, with
" two forks, bearing a fleece of wool and a bottle, was
" carried about with thefe infcriptions—*No Englifh wool*
" *for French wines—Hemp for all thofe who want to foak*
" *their fleeces in claret—No change of ftaple for fpirits.*"

we are directed, in large capitals, to remark, that Hen. Champion, Efq. who oppofes the two *worthy Gentlemen, nominated herein, voted for the Bill of Commerce with France.'* The anxiety previous to the iffue of this event, and the joy on its declaration, were not confined to this Ifland; our factories, both in the Levant and in Portugal, while the Bill was pending, had feconded their petitions, by procuring leave for fome of the principal members of their re- fpective companies, to be admitted into the mercantile committees, and afterwards to fpeak in their behalf at the bar of the Houfe. † Their joy on receiving the news of its ejectment was extravagant, and many days were paffed in feftivity and congratulations. ‡

These particulars, relative to a part of hiftory to which many imperfect allufions have lately

* No. 3421, Sept. 1.

† See the Examination of TORRIANO, an Italian Mer-chant. *Journals,* Vol. XVII.

‡ A Letter from Lifbon, which mentions their rejoicings, fubjoins a curious fact. " Their zeal here for the eject-" ment of the Bill is very extraordinary, for the balance " of trade with your country is certainly much againft " Portugal, who has entailed beggary on her pofterity by " the *Methuen-Treaty*; at the making of which, in one blow, " 100 looms were ruined in one Province." *Flying Poft,* No. 3415. July 17, 1713.

been

been made, I have ftated from the beft authorities, and in the plaineft manner I was able.
Such reflections as have been fuggefted by
them, fall more properly into the other part of
this work ; but even there it is fubmitted to
better judgments to decide how far this event
is applicable or not to the bufinefs now before
the nation.* I now proceed with the review
of England's commerce.

Though

* It may be remarked, that thefe very articles in the
Utrecht Treaty, which raifed fuch a ferment in the nation,
and caufed fo much joy when thrown out of Parliament,
were looked upon, by the Negotiators, in the light of a
great conceffion of France, in confideration of the Englifh
Minifter having given up to her the right of Fifhery at
Newfoundland: But perhaps hiftory cannot fhew ftronger
inftances of chicanery and fineffe, than were exhibited by
France through the whole of this memorable negotiation;
or, on the other hand, more ftriking proofs of the ill effects
of bringing party prejudices into public bufinefs. This,
among many others in the fame collection, is fhewn by the
following letter from Lord Bolingbroke to Mr. Prior,
" Let France depart—the fhameful expedient by which fhe
" thought to bubble us, and all is well ; otherwife, by G—d,
" both they and we are undone. So my Comps. to M. De.
" Torcy, and let him know, that if they do not agree with
" the Queen, I may be a refugee. Do pray make the
" French afhamed of their fneaking chicane. By heaven!
" they treat like pedlars, or, which is worfe, like Attornies."

See

Though the reign of George I. be not remarkable for the profperity either of our foreign
or domeftic trade, yet fome fuccefsful exertions
were then made, the good effects of which became vifible in the fucceeding reign. *The Treaty
of Aix la Chapelle* in 1668, had eftablifhed a good
underftanding between England and Spain,
which, in its confequences, proved highly ferviceable
able to our commerce. Upon this foundation
was raifed a very advantageous Treaty, in the
year 1715, which, notwithftanding the war that
broke out three years after, laid open fome channels of foreign trade which have never fince been
entirely clofed.* The great relief of duties on
the exportation of Britifh manufactures,‡ the
improvements in the iron, brafs, copper, and
filk works, and the liberal bounties for the
encouragement of our Fifheries, are events
which more than compenfate for thofe mad and
fatal delufions, which deform this æra of our

See a *Report of the Committee of Secrecy to the Houfe of Com-
mons,* June 9th, 1715, p. 38, 39, and in the Appendix to the
Report, No. XXII. XXIII. efpecially Lord Bolingbroke's
Letter to De Torcy.

* Treaties of Peace, Vol. I. p. 195.—Vol. II. p. 173.

‡ 8 Geo. I. c. iv.

commer-

commercial hiftory.* Too much caution cannot be ufed in reading the political writings in
the reign which followed, when " not to be
corrupted was the fhame." In this reign
the meaneft artifices of ftatecraft and faction
were oppofed to each other; and, in queftions
of the higheft moment, were fuffered to ufurp
the place of honeft arguments, and rational
deductions. We cannot have a more convincing
proof of this, than by comparing a very popular
work at that day, *On the Caufes of the Decline
of foreign Trade,* written by Sir MATTHEW
DECKER, with the refult of an accurate com-
putation in ANDERSON's *Hiftory of Commerce,*
difpaffionately drawn from the moft authentic
fource. By DECKER we are told, that " under
" the preffure of public debts and taxes, with
" languifhing manufactories, and land every
" day finking in its value, it is not poffible for
" this country long to hold the competition with
" her neighbours."‡ By ANDERSON it appears,
that, juft before the war of 1739, there was every
fymptom of public profperity—Lands at a high

---

* The annual amount of our exports at the peace of
Utrecht was 6,868,480l. At the death of George I. in
1727, it was 7,891,739l.

‡ Quarto Edit. p. 37, 46, 52.

price,

price, and improving—Much induftry and employment—A regular intereft upon money at three *per cent.*——Public credit high, and the tonnage on the commercial fhipping, which, in the beginning of the century, was reckoned at 273,693 tons, and had increafed at the acceffion of Geo. I. to 444,843 tons, but at the clofe of his reign, had funk to 432,832 tons, ftood in the year 1738, at 476,941 tons.* In the year 1728 and 1729, Great Britain had formed Treaties which proved very beneficial to feveral branches of her commerce, by procuring a vent for thofe capitals which had fortunately efcaped the general wreck of project in the preceding reign, and which otherwife might have overcharged fome of the old channels of foreign trade.‡ The war which broke out in 1739, and continued for upwards of nine years, at the fame time that it

* *Hift. of Commerce,* Vol. II. p. 321, 322. See alfo, in the ftrain of Complaint, *Confiderations on the prefent State of Affairs,* by Lord LYTTLETON, publifhed in 1738.

‡ *Collection of Treaties,* V. II. p. 30, and the following. During the three firft years of the reign of Geo. II. the amount of exports was in round numbers, 789,739l. on the annual average; whereas from 1736 to 1739, the *period of impending ruin,* it rofe to 9,992,232l. a difference of more than two millions in favour of this *unfortunate* æra.

gave

gave a check to commerce, afforded ample proof, in the national exertions which it excited, how much our naval and commercial ftrength, as well as internal refources, had been mifrepre-fented ; and, in the fhort interval of peace which fucceeded, trade not only recovered its former level, but rofe to a point of ftill higher eleva-tion.* Thefe are now undifputed teftimonies of increafing opulence ; yet there were then, as in preceding times, able writers, who in bold and pointed terms, pronounced the nation to be on the verge of bankruptcy.‡ Among the many alarms,

* During the war of 1739, the exports had funk to 8,870,499l. At the breaking out of the war of 1755, after fcarcely a feven year's peace, they had rifen to 12,599,112l. Mr. Chalmers obferves, that "on looking over a table of "trade, it appears, that the year of profound peace which "immediately fucceeds a war, always furnifhes a great "exportation, becaufe every merchant makes hafte to be "rich." He inftances the years 1698, 1714, 1749, 1764, 1784, as epochs of great relative commerce. *Eftimate,* &c. p. 214, and his *Chronological Table of Commerce,* oppofite p. 207.

‡ Lord Bolingbroke's *Confiderations on the State of the Nation.* But this "all-accomplifhed ftatefman" had been then too long withdrawn from public life, to form accurate notions on fuch matters, and his peculiar fituation naturally fuggefted fplenetic ones. See alfo DODDINGTON's *Diary,* March 1749, 50, and in the following years.

It

alarms, which it was the fashion of the times to excite on commercial topics, may be reckoned the revival of manufactures and trade in Spain, which a few years before had given rise to despondency and political invective. There was indeed, some ground for the original report.

When the romantic DUKE DE RIPPERDA succeeded the cautious ALBERONI as minister in Spain, he found, it is said, among that statesman's papers, loose memorandums of schemes for the increase of population, and the promotion of national industry. Struck with the general idea, he employed himself, with the assistance of some principal merchants, in digesting a regular plan for that purpose. A Committee was formed to consider on the best means to recover the trade and manufactures of the country. Workmen and artificers were invited from all parts of Europe. Many clothiers and ship-carpenters were allured over from England; and France lost some of her best artists from Lyons. At Segovia and Gaudalaxara, great woollen manufactories were established, and the silk-looms of Valencia,

It is worth remarking, that in the year 1754, by the spirit and liberality of Lord FOLKSTONE, Lord ROMNEY and Dr. STEPH. HALES, *the London Society, for the encouragement of Arts, Manufactures, and Commerce in Great-Britain*, was first established,

Murcia,

Murcia, and Catalonia, already threatened to rival those in the neighbouring provinces of France. In short, were we to judge from a report delivered in by a Spanish Writer at that time, the whole trade of Europe bad fair, in the course of the present century, to fall into the hands of his countrymen.* One fact however is certain, that before the manufactory at Segovia had been three years established, the Duke clothed the Spanish troops from its looms.‡ But, in order to bring these schemes to maturity, the concurrence of the Sovereign was neceſſary; for all commercial concerns are, in Spain, under the direction of the court; and the principal part of the royal revenue ariſes from oppreſſive duties, and exorbitant demands, both on the raw materials and the manufactures of the country. Till these were removed, nothing effectual could be done. This therefore proved an inſurmountable obſtacle; for, as might be expected, the Court abſolutely refuſed to part with any

* Don Jeronimo de Uztariz, cited by Postlethwayte in his *Commercial Intereſt of Great Britain*, who always diſtinguiſhes him by the name of the Patriot-Spaniard, V. II. p. 464.

‡ *Memoirs of the* Duke de Ripperda, p. 100, and the following pages.

of its ancient claims; on the contrary, it
began, in the true spirit of Spanish policy, to
exact heavy subsidies from the newly-elected
manufactories. The moft sanguine promoters
of the commercial reform were difcouraged, and,
ir their difguft, having unguardedly indulged
themfelves in a liberty of fpeech little fuited to
an arbitrary government, they drew down the
difpleafure of the court, both on themfelves
and their projects. This, among other caufes
of difcontent, ended in RIPPERDA's difgrace
and banifhment, and totally extinguifhed all
hopes, that Spain would again become a wealthy and induftrious country. *

The war which broke out in the year
1755, neceffarily threw obftructions in the
way of our foreign commerce, and for a time
damped the ardour of enterprize; yet, even
during this war, after the firft difficulties were
furmounted, trade feems to have recovered its
former tone; for in the year 1760 the value of
exported cargoes was confiderably higher than
it had been in the laft year of the peace. The
Treaty which terminated the war in 1763,

* *Memoirs,* &c. p. 115. His manner of life, and his reflections on the reverfes of his fortune, in his banifhment at
Segovia, are worth confulting.

though

though perhaps it did not hold forth such advantages as from our situation we might reasonably
have expected, yet gave sufficient freedom and
scope to commercial enterprize. * CHALMERS
here gives a very pleasing picture of our opulence, and of the magnificent liberality of our
merchants, who, as he very justly observes,
" literally saved Europe from bankruptcy by
" the superiority of their wealth, and by
" the disinterestedness of their spirit." † For
when all mercantile credit and confidence seemed lost by the great failures at Hamburgh, Ber-
lin, and Holland, the British merchants not
only gave as extensive credit as ever to the unfortunate Houses, but even suspended the pay-
ment of their own acceptances, in order to re-
mit immense sums to relieve the distress of those
commercial cities, and the Bank of England,
when every bill of exchange was doubtful,
still continued to discount them. ‡ When

* In the last year of the Peace, as we have already seen,
our exports were at 12,599,112l. In 1760 they amounted to 14,693,270l. by one account, and by another to
14,694,970l. In 1763, at the Peace of Paris they rose to
14,925,950.

† Estimate, &c. p. 117.

‡ CHALMERS quotes a letter from the Bankers of Hamburgh to the Bankers of Amsterdam, in the Gentleman's
Magazine for the year 1763, p. 422. Estimate, &c. p. 117.

this

this voluntary preffure, fo honourable for a nation to have fuftained, was removed, our foreign and domeftic commerce expanded beyond the example of any former age or country. From the Peace of Paris to the commencement of the late war, nothing was wanted to animate and affift the genius of an active people. Trade, manufactures, agriculture, and every fubordinate department of induftry, were promoted by the wife and patriotic regulations of the Legiflature. Roads and canals were forced over places before deemed impaffable. Waftes were enclofed, marfhes drained, cities adorned, and various other means adopted to facilitate and extend domeftic traffic. On the other hand, by a prudent diftribution of impofts and bounties, many branches of manufactures were relieved, and carried to a point of tafte and refinement, which, notwithftanding their fuperior price, has fecured to them fure and extenfive markets. In fhort, were a period demanded in which the balance of England's trade was moft uniformly in its favour, this undoubtedly muft be named from 1764 to 1774; for in thefe ten years, the two trades of Spain and Portugal only, netted to her a balance of 8,370,131l. Even during the late war, com-

merce

merce did not fuffer fo alarming a depreffion as
might have been expected from fuch an invete-
rate combination againft us. It appears (fays
CHALMERS) that, through the whole courfe
of hoftilities, our traffic never loft its elaftic principle. It had an evident tendency to rife in
1779, till the Spanifh war impofed an additional
burthen; there was a fimilar tendency in 1780,
when the Dutch war added in 1781 no inconfiderable weight; this year, therefore, marks the
loweft degree of its depreffion; but in the following its vigour fprang up, and revived, and
at the clofe of the war exhibited happy fymptoms of that energy which is now every day
more vifibly and extenfively exerted. * The
foregoing review of our commercial ftate at
different periods has no great claim to originality. Its chief merit in many parts is, that of

---

* *Eftimate*, &c. p. 143. In the four years which immediately precede the Colonial war, our exports were at the
average of 15,000,000l. and the net balance in favour of
Britifh commerce was 3,884,844l. In 1781, our exports
had funk to 10,569,187l. In 1784 they were at
14,171,375l. It is a fact worth remarking, that in the war
before laft our commerce was fo far from being embarraffed,
that merchants found it more for their intereft to employ
their capitals in foreign trade than in the Government
loans, to which the Dutch were the principal fubfcribers,
but in the late war the cafe was very different.

being

being a sketch after an admired work of an able
master. *

To correct the pernicious influence of principles which Discontent suggests, and Faction
disseminates, and to awaken a great, but too
easily deluded people to a true sense of their
political consequence (especially in a nation
which has ever been remarked for an unac-
countable propensity to look upon the gloomy
side of events), is surely a laudable and patriotic
undertaking. Such is the object proposed by
the author, to whom I have so often referred
in this latter part of my observations. Beside
the satisfaction which the scholar and politician
must receive from works thus uniting authenti-
city of facts with elegance of language, " The
" Estimate of the comparative Strength of Great

---

* *An Estimate of the comparative Strength of Great Britain,
during the present and four preceding Reigns.* Edit. 1786. By
GEORGE CHALMERS. From the chronological Table of
Commerce inserted in this work, I have, for the most part,
copied the gross amount of our exports at different periods.
As it is vouched by him to be a faithful transcript from the
Ledger of the INSPECTOR GENERAL, to which I had no
opportunities of referring, I apprehend it needs no corro-
borative proof of its fidelity. *Estimate*, p. 218. N. B. I
have omitted the exports of Scotland throughout. They
appear, upon an average of years, to add about one million
to the revenue.

Britain,

" Britain, &c." has this to recommend it at the, prefent hour, that the delineation it contains of our commercial hiftory is as exhilarating as it is faithful. To the name of CHALMERS we ought with gratitude to add thofe of Lord SHEFFIELD and ARTHUR YOUNG, whofe talents are fuccefsfully exerted in fimilar works of genuine patriotifm. * After giving an accurate ftatement of our commercial fituation, YOUNG breaks out in the following manner — " An empire has been rent afunder; " a whole continent, fo peopled as to clafs at " prefent amongft the potentates of the world, " has been detached from Great Britain; and " that event, which was purchafed by the " French, Spaniards, and Dutch, at an expence " of probably more than a hundred and forty " million fterling, as the fureft means of pul- " ling down this country, has been fo far from " having any fuch effect, that we are proved, " on the moft authentic records, to be more " flourifhing, and confequently more formi- " dable, than at any former period fince the " foundation of the monarchy." † To what we muft afcribe this vital ftrength, which nei-

* See Lord SHEFFIELD's *Obfervations on the Commerce of the American States,* 6th Edit. 1784, with an Appendix.

† *Annals of Agriculture,* No. 29, p. 423.

ther

ther war or faction, or the fpirit of luxury, has been able to fubdue, will be obvious on a little reflection. That the fupport was never *tranfat-lantic*, as fome have idly imagined, our prefent commercial fituation fufficiently demonftrates. May we not rather, with an acute Politician of the prefent day, attribute this phænomenon of an almoft uniform fuperiority of our commerce to fomething like the following principles? The fuppreffion of various monopolies and companies of trade at home, and the undermining of their exclufive privileges, or, what is the fame thing, the eluding of their bad effects by means of legal decifions in our courts of law: The nurfing up of new trades, and new branches of commerce, by means of bounties and national premiums: The giving of drawbacks on the exportation of fuch goods as were to have paid a duty if con-fumed at home: The repeal of taxes on raw materials, and on exported manufactures of our country: The improvement of engines, and new difcoveries for the abridgment of labour: The rapid communication by means of roads, canals and pofts: The happy difcoveries in agriculture, and the mechanic arts, the fruits of that patriotic liberality which has been of late fo eminently

* Tucker's *Four Tracts*, p. 213.

G   exerted

exerted among us in public inftitutions, and focieties for the encouragement of induftry and ufeful fkill; and the natural refult of all this national fpirit, the employment of larger capitals in hufbandry and manufactures, and in the importation and exportation of goods; all thefe circumftances co-operating, would render any country rich and flourifhing, whether it had colonies or not.

No wonder then that the Sceptre of commerce continues firm in the hands of a nation where Perfonal Rights are facred, and where every fpecies of Property finds protection and fecurity in the freedom of Civil Government and the equal adminiftration of Law.

THE

THE

A R I F F.

ADVERTISEMENT.

THOUGH the kind communication of fome intelligent manufacturers has put me in poffeffion of materials fufficiently valuable and authentic, I have not, according to my original defign, entered into fuch details as this information would enable me to do; being unwilling to fwell a pamphlet into a volume, with matters known to be *officially* in other hands, much better qualified to lay them before the public. The following Remarks however may not be lefs ufeful, or amufing, though they convey little information that is new to a Statefman or a Politician.

T H E

T A R I F F.

1. THE two High Contracting Parties have thought proper to settle the duties on certain goods and merchandizes, in order to fix invariably the footing on which the trade therein shall be established between the two Nations. In consequence of which they have agreed upon the following TARIFF, viz.

The *Wines* of France, imported directly from France into Great Britain, shall, in no case, pay any higher duties than those which the wines of Portugal now pay.

G 3

The

The Wines of France, imported directly from France into Ireland, shall pay no higher duties than those which they now pay.

2. The Vinegars of France, instead of sixty-seven pounds five shillings and three-pence, and twelve twentieths of a pound sterling per ton, which they now pay, shall not, for the future, pay, in Great Britain any higher duties than thirty-two pounds, eighteen shillings, and ten-pence, and sixteen twentieths of a penny sterling, per ton. *

3. The Brandies of France, instead of nine shillings and sixpence and twelve twentieths of a penny sterling, shall for the future pay, in Great Britain, only seven shillings sterling per gallon, making four quarts, English measure.

4. Oil of Olives, coming directly from

* The present duties on *Vinegars* are for every ton imported 13l. if by strangers, 14l. 10s. by 18 Geo. II. c. ix. By 3 Geo. III. c. xii. an additional duty of 16l. are laid on all French Vinegars, to which 8l. 8s. a ton more are laid by 18 Geo. III. c. xxvii. and another 8l. in addition to this by 20 Geo. III. c. xxx. On home Vinegar, there is for every barrel containing 34 gallons, a duty of 8s. 9d. by 10 and 11 W. III. c. xxi. and by 19 Geo. III. c. xxv. an additional duty of 3 five per cents, which is further regulated by 21 Geo. III. c. xvii. and 22 Geo. III. c. lxvi.— Every maker of Vinegar for sale is required by 24 Geo. III. c. xli. to take out an annual licence of 10l.

France,

France, fhall for the future, pay no higher duties than are now paid for the fame from the
moft favoured nations. *

5. Beer fhall pay reciprocally a duty of thirty
per cent. *ad valorem.* †

6. The

---

* *The Oil of Olives* is that which is moft generally ufed in
Medicine, Food, and *Manufacture.* It appears to have been
brought to great perfection by the ancients. Moft of their
georgical writers have dwelt upon the method of cultivating this fruit, and of preparing it for œconomical ufes.
See COLUMELLA, p. 73, and VARRO, p. 105, in *Scriptores
de Re Ruftica,* edit. 1734. The *Olive* delights in a dry foil,
and thrives in the moft barren fpots, as on the mountains
of Pifa, and the coaft of Genoa, where the eye can difcover
nothing but vaft rocks of ftone ; but it grows beft on gen-
tle hills, defended from North winds and expofed to the
fea air ; though the people of Lucca and Tufcany, by their
extreme induftry, make it fucceed even in low grounds.
Dr. SYMONDS, *on the Soil of Italy,* in YOUNG's *Annals of
Agriculture,* V. II. p. 211. Much of the oil ufed in our
woollen manufactories is from Gallipoli imported hither
immediately from Naples. We take great quantities alfo
from the South of France and from Candia. All *Olive Oils*
imported in foreign fhips, though by Britifh fubjects, are
liable to *Aliens* duty, 12 Car. II. c. xviii. § 9.   BALDWIN
on the *Britifh Cuftoms,* p. 45.

† When goods are to pay *ad valorem,* that value muft be
afcertained by the *two Books of Rates* fet forth by Parliamentary Authority, 12 Car. II. c. iv. and 11 Geo. I. c. vii.

6. The duties on *Hardware, Cutlery, Cabinet Ware*, and *Turnery*, and alſo all works both heavy and light, of Iron, Steel, Copper, and Braſs, ſhall be claſſed; and the higheſt duty ſhall not exceed ten per cent. *ad valorem*.

7. All

or if not rated, by the oath of the importer, or by the price at a public ſale.

It is known that the French make *Beer*, not only with barley, but with wheat, oats, and rye; a ſort made with oats and birch water is ſtrongly recommended in Nephritic caſes. *Philoſ. Tranſ.* No. XCVII. p. 6135. The chief trade of France in this article is domeſtic, namely with Paris, Picardy, and French Flanders. Their duties are regulated by the Tariff of 1664, and are upon exportation, at the rate of 26 ſols the ton, and upon importation 12 ſols the barrel, with an additional rate for England.

By 1 Geo. III. c. vii. ſtrong beer or ale may be exported with an allowance of 8s. the barrel to the brewer by way of drawback. *Hops* are under a variety of reſtrictions in our laws. 9 Ann. c. xii. among other things annexes a penalty of 50l. to the removal of hops before they have been bagged and weighed, and a like penalty on not entering the places of curing and keeping them, with 20l. for concealing hops, as alſo on any brewer who ſhall ſubſtitute any other bitter ingredient. By 10 Geo. III. c. xliv. a penalty of 100l. is inflicted for uſing falſe ſcales and weights. By 14 Geo. III. c. 68. the Officer ſhall forfeit 5l. if he neglect to weigh the bags or pockets, and to mark on them the time, weight or tare, the planter's name and place of abode, and the date of the year in which

7. All forts of Cottons, * manufactured in the dominions of the two Sovereigns in Europe, and alfo Woollens, whether *knit* or *wove*, including *Hofiery*, fhall pay, in both countries, an *import duty* of twelve per cent. *ad valorem* ; all manufactures of Cotton or Wool, mixed with Silk, excepted, which fhall remain prohibited on both fides.

8. Cambrics and Lawns † fhall pay, in both countries, an import duty of five fhillings

or

which fuch hops were grown. The altering, forging, or obliterating of fuch mark incurs a penalty of 10l. By a late act, five per cent. is added to the other duties on hops:

* We have an account of the induftry of the town of Manchefter as early as the year 1641. "The town of Manchefter buys linen yarn of the Irifh in great quantities, and weaving it, returns the fame again in linen; neither doth her induftry reft here, for fhe buys cotton-wool in London, that comes from Cyprus and Smyrna, and works it into fuftians, vermillions, dimmities, &c." Lewis Roberts, *Treafure of Traffic.* There is a great cotton manufactory at Rouen in Normandy. It was with concern, that in the year 1784, I heard of feveral Englifhmen employed there, two of whom had worked for 13 years at Manchefter. Cotton works have, within thefe few years, been eftablifhed, with fuccefs, both in Ireland and Scotland.

† By 32 Geo. II. no *Cambrics* or *French Lawns* fhall

be

or six livres Tournois, per demi piece of seven yards and three quarters, English measure; and linens made of flax or hemp, manufactured in the dominions of the two Sovereigns in Europe, shall pay no higher duties, either in Great Britain or France, than linens manufactured in Holland or Flanders, imported into Great Britain, now pay.

And Linens made of flax or hemp manufac-

be imported, unless they be packed in bales, cases, or boxes, covered with sackcloth or canvas, containing each 100 whole pieces. These shall be imported only for exportation, to be lodged in the King's warehouses, and not to be delivered out but under the like security and restrictions as prohibited East-India goods: and no customs or duties whatever shall be paid or secured thereon, other than half the old subsidy, which is to remain by law after the goods are exported. Other restrictions on the importation, the wearing and the selling of foreign *Cambrics* and *Lawns* are to be found in 18 Geo. II. c. xxxvi.—21 Geo. II. c. xxvii. —4 Geo. III. c. xxxvii.—and 7 Geo. III. c. xliii. We are at present supplied from the manufactories of Ireland and Scotland. It may be questioned, whether those countries will long find it their interest to promote such fabrics as *Cambric*, *Lawn*, or *Gauze*, to the check of their linen works, for it seems like preferring a precarious article of manufacture to one which is secure. It is said, that there are in Glasgow alone more than 1000 *Muslin* looms. St. Quentin and Cambray are as principal manufactories for all these articles as any in France.

tured

tured in Ireland or France, fhall reciprocally pay no higher duties than linens manufactured in Holland, imported into Ireland, now pay.

9. *Sadlery* fhall reciprocally pay an impoft duty of fifteen per cent. ad valorem.

10. Gauzes of all forts fhall reciprocally pay ten per cent. ad valorem.

11. Millinery made up of Muflin, Lawn, Cambric, or Gauze of every kind, or of any other article admitted under the prefent *Tariff*, fhall pay reciprocally a duty of twelve per cent. ad valorem ; and if any articles fhall be ufed therein, which are not fpecified in the Tariff, they fhall pay no higher duties than thofe paid for the fame articles by the moft favoured Nations.

12. *Porcelain, Earthen-ware* and *Pottery*, fhall pay reciprocally twelve per cent. ad valorem.

13. *Plate-glafs*, and Glafs-ware in general, fhall be admitted on each fide, paying a duty of twelve per cent. ad valorem.*

CUSTOMS.

* Moft of the duties on Glafs granted by 19 Geo. II. c. xii. were repealed by an act paffed in 1777, and the following duties impofed ; for all plate enamel, ftained and pafte glafs, and on all window glafs, and every other kind of white glafs, the fum of one fhilling and four pence the
pound

C U S T O M S.

A fuccinct and general account of the CUS-
TOMS neceffarily claims a place in a work of this
nature.

Though the firft *formal* Eftablifhment of
CUSTOMS and duties on the imports and exports of this kingdom occur in the reign of
EDWARD I. yet by that very act we are informed
of their prior exiftence. At the opening of the
fourteenth century, this King, upon confideration
of the many immunities and privileges granted
by him to foreign merchants, refiding in and
pound weight; and for all green glafs in bottles, four
fhillings for every dozen of quarts; and for materials ufed
in the manufacture of plate and phial glafs, eighteen fhillings
and eight pence the cwt. for making of broad window glafs,
feven fhillings cwt. for making of crown glafs, fourteen
fhillings cwt. and for common bottles, &c. three fhillings
and fix-pence cwt.

Few manufactures require a larger capital or greater
profits to fupport it, than this; for a fingle furnefs cofts
£3500, and is five or fix years in building; befide fuch
accidents as in many other branches are immaterial, are in
this of the higheft confequence, for merely the burfting of
a pot of glafs in the fire, will often incur a lofs of £250.

France has nine principal Glafs Works, five of which are
in the foreft of Lyons, the other four in the diftrict of Eu,
at Beaumont, near Rouen, and in Rue St. Antoine, at
Paris. Our principal Plate Glafs manufacture is near
Prefcot in Lancafhire.

4   trading

trading with this ifland, *by the advice and confent of his Parliament*, publifhed a declaration of thefe privileges, annexing as the price of his protection certain *Cuftoms* and *Duties* to be paid by them on merchandizes either imported or exported.*

GILBERT conceives thefe privileges to have confifted chiefly in having the full ufe of the King's warehoufes, weights, meafures, &c.‡ This royal declaration is called CHARTA MERCATORIA,§ and may be confidered as containing the fimple elements of that very intricate fyftem of impofts, which has been gradually accumulating ever fince, to the great hindrance and confufion of commerce.

It is unneceffary here to enumerate the feveral fpecies which arofe between that æra and the great Statute of 12 Carol. II. c. iv. which eftablifhed the fubfidy of tonnage and poundage, or as it is more technically called, the Old Subfidy, which is the foundation of our prefent *Cuftoms* ; neither is it the prefent purpofe to dwell

---

* RYMER'S *Fædera*, Tom. III. fol. 269. See the anfwer given by Edward II. to Philip the Fair, upon his requefting to have French Merchants releafed from a certain duty.

‡ Hiftory of the Exchequer, p. 214.

§ *Fædera*, Tom. IV. fol. 361.

on the difpute whether or not the Cuftoms be part of the revenue of the Crown by *Common Law :* a point which, above all others, contributed to thofe violent ftruggles between prerogative and privilege at the beginning of the laft century.*

I fhall only obferve that it appears from *Magna Charta* that certain cuftoms, as on Wool, Woolfells, and Leather, were paid to the Crown, previoufly to any act of parliament. Still the right has conftantly been difputed, and the rolls of parliament fwarm with inftances of proteftations againft it. BLACKSTONE thinks that SIR EDWARD COKE has plainly fhewn that the King's firft claim to Cuftoms was by *Grant of Parliament*, 3 Edward I.† which probably alludes to that very event already mentioned, as the firft *formal* eftablifhment of our Cuftoms; and HALE fays, even of *Prifage* (a duty peculiarly belonging to the Crown) " That is a " cuftom fettled in the Crown by *Common Law*,

---

* See a fketch of thefe ftruggles prefixed to the celebrated *Cafe of Impofitions* in *State Trials*, Vol. XI. It may here be remarked, that the act which granted the duties of tonnage and poundage after the Reftoration, has thefe cautious words : "No rates can be impofed on merchandizes " imported or exported by fubjects or aliens, but, by *Confent* " *of Parliament*." 12 Carol. II. c. iv. fec. 6.

† Commentaries, B. I. c. viii.

" yet

" yet not fo infeparable from the Crown, nor fo
" perfonal to the King, but it may be difcharged
" or transferred."†

The following are the principal branches of
our prefent Cuftoms.

1. The OLD SUBSIDY, which confifts of a
tonnage duty on Wines imported, and a poundage duty on other goods imported.

2. PETTY CUSTOMS or ALIENS DUTY,
payable by Merchant-Strangers on all goods
imported, which are liable to the fubfidy of
poundage.

3. ADDITIONAL DUTY on tonnage and
poundage added to the former.

4. ONE PER CENT. INWARDS, payable upon
all *imports to Great Britain, from any place of the
Mediterranean Sea,* beyond the port of Malaga,
in any veffel that hath not two decks, fixteen
guns, and the proportion of two men to each
gun.

5. COMPOSITION ON PETTY SEIZURES.
The moiety paid to the Crown by the Commiffioners of the Cuftoms for feizures under the

† See a Treatife lately publifhed in HARGRAVE's *Law
Tracts,* from a MS. of Lord Chief Juftice HALE, in three
parts, the laft of which treats with great legal erudition on
" The Cuftoms of Goods imported and exported."

value

value of forty fhillings, for which they are allowed to compound.

Thefe five only, in the ftrict fenfe of the revenue laws, are properly called THE CUSTOMS. There are however various others by the names of Impofts on Wines, Vinegar, Tobacco, Coinage, Duties, Excife, &c. whence the Crown revenue arifes; though moft of the diftinctions are now dropped, except by the officers immediately concerned, their produce being all blended together under the one denomination of THE CUSTOMS.* We may obferve that originally thefe duties were levied both on importation and exportation, but for many years, with few exceptions, the new Cuftoms have been raifed on importations only.

The ftatute of 12 Carol. II. c. iv. eftablifhes two very plain fyftems. By the one a fpecific fum is charged on a certain quantity, a ton of wine, for example; by the other, rates or imaginary values are annexed to all other goods of common importation, and a proportional duty is levied on each article. Had the fimplicity of this plan been ftrictly followed in all fubfequent impofts, that confufion and inequa-

* CUNNINGHAM's *Hiftory of Taxes*, p. 88, and the following. BLACKSTONE's *Comment*. B. I. c. viii.

lity

lity which prevails in our Cuſtoms would have been avoided ; but this is ſo far from being the caſe, that even in leſs than twelve years from the publication of this act, the legiſlature began to deviate from its principles, and, regardleſs of the original rates therein annexed, charged ſeveral articles according to their meaſure and weight.*
Since that time almoſt every ſtatute which has added a freſh duty, has unavoidably increaſed the perplexity. " It were to be wiſhed (ſays the " laſt compiler of our cuſtoms) that the whole " of our impoſts had been framed upon a more " uniform plan, and that both the convenience " and beauty of ſyſtem had been preſerved. But " the defect cannot now be eaſily removed."‡
The great extent of the *Books of Rates,*§ and the want of perſpicuity in the arrangement, calls aloud

---

* 22 Carol. II. c. iv.   25 Carol. II. c. vii.

‡ BALDWIN in the preface to his *Survey of Britiſh Cuſtoms,* &c. p. 4.

§ The Cuſtoms are chiefly contained in two books of Rates, ſet forth by Parliamentary authority ; one by 12 Carol. II. c. iv. the other by 11 Geo. I. c. vii. It was to the liberality, no leſs than to the perſeverance of the Houſe of Peers, that the public were at laſt indebted in 1696, for the eſtabliſhment of the *Inſpector General* of the imports and exports, and for the *Cuſtom-houſe Ledger,* which contains the particulars and value of both, and which forms there-

H   fore

aloud for an attempt at reformation. The perſon who ſhall engage in ſuch a taſk, I would wiſh to remind of what the great Financier of France has obſerved on the ſame perplexed ſtate in which he found the fiſcal legiſlation of his country. "This ſtrange arrangement of our " cuſtoms," ſays he, "has abſolutely ſupported " itſelf by its own defects ; the multiplicity of " particular caſes, the accumulation of rules, the " confuſion of principles ; in ſhort, all that " antique contexture woven into ſo many knots, " has conſtantly preſented the idea of an im- " menſe enterpriſe, whenever attempts have " been made to proceed to a reform, by ſtudying " *details* : But when I took a contrary method, " by making myſelf maſter of the *whole collec-* " *tively by reflection,* and by taking pains to " diſcern the principle diviſions, and the *ele-* " *ments,* as well as the *reſults* of each, the whole " affair became ſimplified."* As great a ſource of confuſion and inequality as any, is, the great

fore the moſt uſeful record, with regard to trade, that any country poſſeſſes. CHALMERS's *Eſtimate of the Com- parative Strength,* &c. pref. p. 7.

* NECKER's *Adminiſtration of the Finances,* V. II. p. 167, of MORTIMER's Tranſlation. This miniſter's plan is a beautiful example of Analyſis, for the imitation of a ſtateſman in any department.

difference which often fubfifts between the *real*
and the *nominal* value of duties on foreign articles. When the rates were affixed in the reign
of Charles II. they were then equal to the *real*
values, but fince that time, the decline of the
value of money, with other caufes, has contributed to raife the *prices* above the *rates*, infomuch that often when the duties are 25 or 26
per cent. on the *rates*, this will not be more than
7 or 8 per cent. on the *real value*. In the
article of linens this is obvioufly the cafe, and it
caufed no fmall contradictions in the reports and
opinions on that manufacture, when it was taken
into confideration by parliament fome few years
ago.

The bulk as well as the form of our Cuftoms
has been alfo a fubject of complaint to fome
writers on commercial politics. The duties on all
exports of Britifh Manufacture, except on fome
few articles which were regarded as *materials*, were
removed in the year 1722, but no relief was
given to imports ; on the contrary, they have,
in moft inftances, been gradually burthened with
new duties. Thefe high and numerous impofts,
it has been thought, are attended with many
evils in fuch a country as England. Among
the principal perhaps may be reckoned a check

on

on the increafe of capitals, and the poffible improvements of manufactories; an encouragement
to fmuggling, and above all, by enhancing the
price of articles neceffary in the conftruction and
fitting out of fhips, as hemp, flax, iron, &c. the
confequent difcouragement to navigation and
commerce. I have chofen thefe inftances,
becaufe it is by a fuperiority in them that our
mercantile fyftem is characterized; and were
fuch falutary reliefs permitted to co-operate with
this national fpirit, it is not eafy to conceive what
might in time be the extent and perfection of
our foreign trade and domeftic induftry. Mr.
Locke was ever of opinion that high duties
encouraged rather than depreffed the confumption of foreign commodities. " The emulation,"
fays he, " ever is, who fhall have the fineft,
" that is, the deareft things, not the moft con-
" venient or ufeful. How many things do we
" value and buy becaufe they come at dear rates
" from Japan and China, which, if they were
" our own manufacture or produce, would be
" contemned or neglected ? Have not feveral of
" our commodities offered to fale been defpifed,
" and the very fame eagerly bought for
" French at a double price ? You muft not
" think therefore that the raifing their price will

" leffen

" leſſen the vend of faſhionable foreign com-
" modities among us, but rather increaſe it :"*
and DE WITT in his Memoirs purſues preciſely
the ſame train of argument ;‡ which ſeems
confirmed by an obſervation of GEE, on the
faſhion of preferring French Wines, after the
duties were laid on at the latter end of the laſt
century : for, ſays he " though they were raiſed
" to £80 per ton, or more, ſome particular im-
" porters choſe rather to keep up thoſe high
" prices than to have them cheaper ; and being
" aſked why they thus choſe to keep up the
" prices, they anſwered, that gentlemen would
" not think it good unleſs it coſt 5 or 6 ſhillings
" a flaſk."† It is true indeed, that impoſts may
be carried ſo far as to become prohibitions, and
in that caſe alſo they might be as prejudicial as in
the other; for as ſays SWIFT humorouſly, " in the
" Arithmetic of the Cuſtoms, *two* and *two* do
" not always make *four*, but often only ONE."

It is not on foreign Articles alone that many
Writers on finance have argued for the relief

* LOCKE's *Conſiderations on Trade*, &c. p. 93, and again
p. 116.

‡ Edit. Ratiſbon, p. 77. Dr. SMITH computes that
taking together all the reſtraints upon French goods at the
commencement of the late war, they muſt have amounted to
75 per cent.

† *Trade conſidered*, &c. p. 141.

H 3   of

of Cuftoms. The exportation of domeftic commodities, notwithftanding much beneficial reform, has been oppreffed by them. It will be faid, perhaps, that in moft cafes *Drawbacks* have been applied to counteract the effects of thefe duties; but, befide the injudicious mode often of applying them, the policy of the meafure itfelf (except in the cafe of foreign goods imported for re-exportation) may be queftioned. The various frauds practifed in this line frequently brings a certain lofs on the revenue, without either altering or extending the ftate of the Trade; for it is a known fact, that this mode of encouraging commerce and manufactures alone amounts to near a million a year. * It was ever confidered as the moft prudent plan in fifcal police, and as fuch was, as we have feen, in a great meafure adopted in this country, to difcharge all Cuftoms payable on domeftic manufactures at their exportation, and alfo on the raw materials ufed in them at their importation. By the firft, the merchant will be encouraged to fend more goods on better terms abroad; and by the laft, the manufacturer will be enabled to fell cheaper at home.

W I N E S.

Before the Revolution, the Æra of thofe mer-

* Young's *Annals of Agriculture*, &c. No. I. p. 44.

cantile jealoufies between France and England, which gave rife to the monopolizing fyftem of reftrictions and prohibitions, the Wines of Bourdeaux and Languedoc were fold in London at eighteen and twenty pounds a Ton, and more than two-thirds of the confumption through the whole Kingdom was imported in Englifh bottoms. * But in the year 1713, in confequence of heavy duties, their price had rifen to nine fhillings the gallon, which, according to a regulation of 5 Anne, ch. xxvii. fixing the Wine Ton at 252 gallons, amounts to 113l. 8s. the Ton. †

From general obfervation it appears, that the moft thriving, and the richeft-flavoured Vineyards, are thofe fituated between the 40th and 50th degrees. In thefe latitudes, we find Portugal, Spain, France, Switzerland, Italy, Hungary, part of Greece, and the Southern Circles of Germany, countries which undoubtedly produce excellent Wines. For general ufe, thofe of France have ever been preferred; and among them, the Wines of Burgundy, Champagne, and the neighbourhood of Vienne, are efteemed the beft. I fhall readily be ex-

* DAVENANT's *Political Works*, V. III. p. 146. Edit. 1723.

† A weekly Paper of that day, called the *Briftol Poft-Boy*, No. 625.

cufed

culed reciting the long catalogue of names by
which they are diftinguifhed, when it is known,
that the province of Burgundy alone produces
eighteen or twenty different forts: they ufually
receive their titles either from the fpot of cultivation, or the various modes of preparing the
liquor. The Wines of the fouthern provinces
are of a ftronger body than thofe made in other
parts of the kingdom; Languedoc, in particular, produces a fort which has all the fulnefs of
the Portugal grape, with a very fuperior flavour,
and is purchafed in the country for about
12 l. the Ton. Bourdeaux, Rochelle, Nantes,
Rouen, Marfeilles, Toulon, are the principal
places where the Wines of France are fhipped
for exportation, and it is calculated that near
6000 Tons are fent annually to England from
Bourdeaux alone. According to the ftatement
of Mr. NECKER, France exports yearly, in
Wines and Brandies, to the value of 1,640,625 l. *
yet it is well underftood that this branch of
trade, under proper regulations, might ftill be
confiderably increafed. At prefent, befide the
original expences of the land, and the neceffary
cofts of preparing its produce, the proprietor of
a Vineyard is chargeable with heavy duties at
every ftep he takes towards exportation; the

* *Adminiftration of Finance,* &c. V. II. p. 117.

conveyance of the Wine to Bourdeaux, a Commiffion to the boat-mafter upon its receipt and
delivery, Fees to the officers for affixing the town
mark, and certain port duties before the goods
can be difcharged, or the bill of freight delivered.
Notwithftanding thefe difadvantages, there
are circumftances which render this fpecies
of property in France more eligible than moft
others. It was not, as fome imagined, becaufe
the land was unfit for any other purpofe, that
the proportion of Vineyards had fo much increafed fome years ago as to require an edict to
reftore fuch eftates as had been purchafed and
planted, to their original cultivation; for it was
found that much land, which had produced excellent crops of corn, was at that time converted
into Vineyards. It is very natural to prefer a
fpecies of property which is free and fecure, to
one which is cafual and reftricted. Property in
Wine, by reafon of the perfon who holds it being
at liberty either to ftore it up, or to carry it to a
home or a foreign market, has, in France, thefe
advantages over property in *Corn*. Befide, with
very few exceptions, the Wine-trade is not like
that of Corn, entangled with monopolies, fo
that the expences and rifk of cultivation, at
leaft, are anfwered by the competition of pur-
chafers. Contrary alfo to the cuftom on eftates
in Corn lands, the proprietor of a Vineyard
usually

nfually keeps it in his own hands, and as fuch a ftock, as would be neceffary in the manage-ment of a farm is never required in a Vineyard, he thence derives an obvious advantage; for, as it has been obferved, while thofe who are employed in its cultivation fometimes want even the neceffaries of life, the landlord makes from three to five pounds an acre.

It fhould appear that the cultivation of Vineyards has proved in France very favourable to population; for it has been afferted, that the fame fpace which, in a Corn country, employs 1400 perfons, requires more than 2600 when planted with Vines. * If this be really the cafe, would it not fhew more wifdom in the French Government, if inftead of iffuing Edicts for *difvineyarding* large tracts of country, it would turn its attention towards a removal of the unmerciful reftrictions, both upon the tranfportation and exportation of Corn? † This, by laying open a larger market for the vend of the commodity, would induce many to fet their hands heartily to the plough, and by lowering the price of grain, would enable the peafantry to live lefs wretchedly than they do at prefent.

* BEAUSOBRE, *Etude de la Politique*, &c. Tom. I. p. 51.

† This was in fome meafure done in 1768, but not in a manner fufficiently liberal to produce its full effect.

By

By fuch a meafure, the increafe of farms would, it is highly probable, be fo far from diminifhing the number or extent of Vineyards, that it would rather encourage and improve them ; with this difference, perhaps, that many fertile fpots, now mifapplied to the culture of the vine, would be feen bearing plentiful harvefts of grain, while the barren heaths of Guienne, the mountains of Auvergne, and other unprofitable parts of the country, would be glowing with luxuriant vintages. This reciprocal benefit is actually feen to take place, in fome inftances, even under the prefent regulations; for it is remarked, that Corn is no where better cultivated in France, than in the richeft Wine provinces.

Befide the advantage that France will derive from England, fhould the prefent Treaty take effect, a large market is now open to her Wines in America, which hitherto was fupplied chiefly from Madeira, Lifbon, and Fayal, unlefs indeed this extenfive country fhould fucceed in cultivating the vine in fome of her fouthward provinces. This is far from being improbable, when we recollect the refult of an experiment once made there. " Between thirty and forty years ago, a " provincial act paffed in South Carolina, by " which a bounty of 60l. proclamation-money " was to be given to any perfon that fhould " produce a pipe of found merchantable Wine,

" made

" made from vines of the growth of the colony.
" A man of the name of Thorpe did receive
" the bounty for three pipes; his Vineyard was
" within thirty miles of Charles-Town, and was
" under the care of a certain Portuguefe pro-
" cured for the purpofe, but at his death the
" land was converted to other ufes." * Lord
SHEFFIELD is of opinion notwithftanding, that
America is never likely to be a good Wine
country; but fhould this really prove to be the
cafe, it will be owing to other caufes than defects either of foil or climate, principally perhaps to that preference which is at prefent given
to the cultivation of rice and tobacco. But
how, it may be afked, is England likely to be
affected by fuch a revolution in the ftate of
French agriculture, and fo wide an extenfion
of the Wine trade? Without adverting to the
common, but very juft argument on the fuperior advantage which every commercial country
ought to obtain from rich and induftrious competitors over one whofe cuftomers are poor and
indolent, let it be remembered, that fair competition muft, in every point of view, be a fpur
to induftry; in any fingle branch of trade its

* Lord SHEFFIELD's *Obfervations on the Commerce of the American States*, p. 56, a Note.

good

good effects are foon vifible among that particular clafs of merchants or manufacturers; but
when it is encouraged between different departments of trade, it then becomes manifeft in the
general induftry and opulence of a nation. The
fame reafoning may be applied to the cafe of
two neighbouring kingdoms, where a competition, efpecially of the latter fort, muft naturally
tend to increafe the demand and improve the
quality of thofe articles in which they refpec-
tively excel. There is not much caufe, therefore, for England's jealoufy at any increafe of
demand on the vintages of France. What lofs
does the woollen-draper fuftain by the improving trade of his neighbour the wine-merchant?
Has he not rather caufe to rejoice in an event
which, by furnifhing the whole neighbourhood
with a richer cuftomer, muft neceffarily bring
into his hands fome fhare of his fuccefs? In the
fame manner both reafon and experience fhould
teach us, that from this dreaded extenfion of
the Wine-trade of France, our own ftaple commodities will neceffarily derive many future
benefits in the woollen, iron, and hard-ware
manufactories. But, it is urged, this is not the
only objection—Portugal is a better cuftomer
than France, and therefore we ought in return
to deal with her in preference. Suppofe, for a
moment,

moment, that this were a fact, " Are the fneak-
" ing arts of underling tradefmen to be thus
" erected into political maxims for the conduct
" of a great empire?" * A liberal trader pur-
chafes at the cheapeft and beft market, with no
regard to fuch little interefts as this. It appears, however, from undeniable proofs, that
our favourite trade with Portugal has long been
on the decline, and gradually turning more and
more againft us for almoft thefe laft thirty years.
At prefent our exports to that country fcarcely
amount, upon an average of ten years, (except
during the fhort fpace of our late Spanifh hoftilities, which naturally caufed them to increafe)
to one half of what they did in the year 1760. †
The fact is, the interchange of the two countries was never fettled upon a fair and equal
foot of reciprocity, and the Portuguefe thus
taking advantage of an original defect in the
Methuen-Treaty, have allowed the woollen manufactures of other countries to compete with
ours in their markets. In the article of linens

* Smith's *Wealth of Nations*, B. IV. ch. iii.

† Where the imports are materials for manufacture, a
trade may be confiderably againft a country, and yet be,
upon the whole, a beneficial one. This was the cafe with
our Ruffia trade; but it does not hold good in the prefent
inftance of our intercourfe with Portugal.

they

they have decidedly given the preference to
France; and as to our cottons, they have put
them under an abfolute prohibition. The
clamours that have conftantly been raifed on
every attempt in this country to reduce the
enormous duties on French Wines, and the
threats of Portugal to withdraw from a Treaty
fhe has fo palpably violated, ought furely to
give us no alarm; the prefent effects of that
Treaty will not juftify it. But what would be
the confequence fuppofing thefe threats to be
actually executed, and the prohibitions on both
fides eftablifhed? Why, clearly this; that Portugal has effectually loft a market for near
12,000 tons annually of fuch Wines as no other
country will purchafe of her; while the fuperior
quality and cheapnefs of our woollens muft fecure
them a market any where, and " probably
" under another name, and by another channel,
" even in Portugal itfelf." *

BRAN-

* Lord SHEFFIELD, to whofe excellent writings I am
indebted for the above remark, has in a clear manner
fhewn, that in Ireland the confumption of Portugal Wine
has greatly increafed within thefe laft twenty years, and
that French Wines have proportionably diminifhed. (*Obfervations, Americ. Comm.* in the Appendix, p. 291) Ireland
exports to Portugal camblets and butter; her woollens were
not included in the Treaty of 1703. The preference the

hn

BRANDIES.

The *Wine Brandy* of France is, in the higheft eftimation, and by a decree of Parliament in the year 1699, this is the only fort permitted to be fold in Paris, under a heavy penalty.

The provinces of Poictou, Anjou, Touraine, Orleans, and the diftrict of Nantes produce the beft that is applied to home-confumption; the different kinds for exportation are made in Bourdeaux, Cogniac, Charente, Burgundy, and Champagne; though the aforenamed provinces of Poictou, &c. fupply a great deal alfo for this purpofe. Brandies, indeed, are made in almoft all the wine countries, though it is obferved, that the fuperior wines make the worft; accordingly in many places they only apply them to this fervice when they are pricked, or otherwife injured. The rich-flavoured vintages of Greece, and of the fouthward parts of Italy, afford very little Brandy, and of an inferior quality: the yearly export of this article

has lately given to the Portuguefe Wines, is with a view of being put on a foot, in this refpect, with great Britain; and there is reafon to think, that fhe is able to reap confiderable benefit from fuch an admiffion. Her exports to Portugal in 1783, were 174,493l. her imports, 92000l. and it is faid thefe were paid for by her exported Butter alone.

from

from France is computed at more than half a million sterling; * at the latter end of the last century, when the duty was no more than 9l. a ton, this country imported annually upwards of 6000 tons; † in consequence of the high duties at present subsisting, the consumption has long been diminished, and upon an average of late years the quantity imported has sunk three fifths. The merchants of Rochelle and Nantes seldom freight a ship either for America, Africa, or the North Seas, without making Brandy a part of the cargo. We receive a considerable quantity of our consumption through the hands of the Dutch, who carry on an extensive trade with France in this article. It has been a received opinion, that although neither English malt or molasses spirit have ever been brought to the perfection of Wine-Brandy, yet the fault is not so much in the grain or fruit whence the extract is made, as in the manner of preparation. Both grapes and grain have the same principles of oil, salt, phlegm and earth, and differ only in the quantity and connection of those principles. A patent, not many years ago, was obtained for making Brandy

* NECKER's *Administration of Finance*, Vol. II. p. 207.

† *Considerations on Trade*, &c. in the year 1724.

I   from

from carrots and parfnips; the latter, it was found, after a variety of curious experiments, made a liquor very nearly refembling the Wine-Brandy.

If the motives for complaint be exactly ftated, it is not without reafon, that our Weft-India merchants have taken alarm at the reduction of duties on this article, imported from France, as propofed in the Tariff. From the memorial prefented by them to the Minifter, the refult of their meetings, and the opinion of intelligent individuals on the fubject, the following appears to be the fum of their apprehenfions and their wifhes.

They requeft that the *Rum* of the Britifh Weft-India Iflands fhould be put upon the fame foot with regard to the *Brandies* of France, that the wines of Portugal are to the wines of France; for, unlefs fuch a proportionate adjuftment of duties take place, the fale of a foreign produce will be encouraged to the detriment, and perhaps the ruin, of what may be termed a domeftic one. It is well known that Rum muft pay more freight from the place of production than Brandy, and that it fuffers more by leakage and evaporation, requires larger capital, and from the nature of the trade renders the merchant liable to greater lofs

of

of interest upon it. This, among other instances, might be exemplified in several late obstructions of the intercourse between the Islands and North America, which, to the great disadvantage of the trader, must necessarily always turn the superfluous Rum into the British market. It appears moreover, that while these obstructions have risen in this staple of West-India trade, the French have been industriously facilitating the vend of their brandies by a variety of regulations. That the interests of the sugar-trade are so naturally connected with those of Rum, that whatever impedes the one must injure the other. * That this trade is of no small assistance to the marine skill and spirit of Great Britain, by reason of the length of the voyage and the number of British ships and seamen employed in it, whereas the Brandy-trade will be carried on in short trips between England and France, with a large proportion of French vessels and crews. That on this account, added to the consideration that prime cost, freight and insurance are all higher, the quantity of Rum smuggled from the West-Indies is very small, compared with that of

---

* It is said the Rum insures to the planter the expences and casualties of the sugar; and they reckon, that each hogshead of sugar produces from 40 to 60 gallons of Rum.

Brandies

Brandies from France ; the duties therefore on the former are more faithfully collected. That as the prime cost of Brandy in France is upon the average 1s. 2½d. a gallon, and that of Rum 2s. 4d. in order to preserve a just proportion in the reduction of the duties on each, if those on Brandies, as proposed in the Tariff, be lowered two shillings and sixpence the gallon, those on Rum should be lowered one shilling and nine pence. *

Such appear to be the principal grounds of complaint from this respectable body of merchants, whose remonstrance, there is little doubt, will have its due weight in the deliberations of Parliament, especially when it is considered also what an injury our home-distilleries may receive by precipitately exposing them to an unequal competition. Will it not, moreover, admit of a doubt, whether the proposed rate of reduction of the duties on French Brandies be sufficient to prevent smuggling, for even the duty of 7s. the gallon, is almost 500 per cent. on the prime cost, and whether by such an ineffectual reduction of the duties, the revenue will not sustain a considerable loss with-

* See "the Memorial of the General Meeting of the West-India Merchants and Planters," presented to the Lords Commissioners of the Treasury.

out any adequate compenfation or advantage to
the public. *

IRON, STEEL, and COPPER.

There is fcarcely any branch of manufacture
in which labour and ingenuity are feen to add
more to the original value of materials than in
that of Iron and Steel; of this the beautiful fabrics of Birmingham and Sheffield afford numerous examples, and it is equally as evident in
the ftupendous foundries at Carron and Colebroke Dale, as in the minuteft operation of the

* The principal laws which regulate the duties on the
importation of Brandies, are 7 and 8 W. III. c. xx. laying a duty of 30l. the ton on fingle, and 60l. the ton on
double proof, repealed by 6 Geo. II. c. xvii. § 2; which,
inftead of it, levies an excife of 1s. for every gallon of
fingle proof, to be paid by the importer before landing,
over and above all other duties, and of 2s. on double proof.
See, alfo 2 W. and M. c. ix. § 12. 12 W. III. c. xi.
§ 8. 3 Ann. c. iv. v. 5 Ann. c. xix. made perpetual by
1 Geo. I. c. xii. 6 Geo. I. c. xxi. § 12. 8 Geo. I. c. xviii.
§ 11. 6 Geo. III. c. xlvii. The act paffed 1 W. and M.
c. xxxiv. which entirely prohibits the importation of French
goods, appears by the preamble to have been intended principally for the encouragement of the home diftilleries;
this is the more probable, becaufe in the following year a
heavy duty was laid on the exportation of corn. 2 W. and
M. c. ix.

workfhops

workſhops at Saliſbury and Woodſtock. In
reflecting on the various applications of theſe
metals to agricultural, naval, military, mecha-
nical, and œconomical purpoſes, we are immediately ſtruck with their extenſive utility and
importance, and are abſolutely loſt in amaze-
ment, when we attempt to trace them through
all their gradations and forms, from the cannon
or the anchor to the lancet or the watch-ſpring.
Though iron ore is known to be very plentiful
in this kingdom, it is not poſſible to aſcertain,
with any accuracy, what proportion of the product is worked up, becauſe it is not only in-
termixed with foreign iron, but is very com-
monly concealed under a foreign name. In
the year 1719, when a bill " for extending the
laws concerning the importation of naval ſtores
from the Britiſh American Colonies," was agi-
tated, it was computed that *two thirds* of what
was conſumed in this kingdom, was imported
from Sweden and Ruſſia. * It appears, that on
an average of ten years, our trade in this article with the Baltic may be reckoned at 27,500
tons, value 314,000l.

In the year 1749 another bill was propoſed
for encouraging the importation of bar-iron

* GEE, *Trade conſidered*, p. 16.

from

from America, in the courfe of which the fpirit
of monopoly defcended to very fhameful expe-
dients, to prevent its taking effect. Among
other things it was boldly afferted, that American Iron was of a quality very inferior to Swe-
difh, though by the *Officer's Reports*, then prefented to the Houfe, it was fhewn that various
experiments made a few years before, in the
King's dock-yards, had proved it in all refpects
of equal goodnefs. It was alfo urged, that if
we withdrew from the iron trade of the Baltic,
we muft forego the advantages of importing
their hemp and flax; but the event, as far as
it was tried, did not juftify fuch apprehenfions. *
The fact was, their fears were of a more felfifh
nature. The proprietors of our iron-foundries
knew it was not for their intereft that an event
fhould take place, which would lower the price
of the metal, and thus by a narrow-minded policy
they attempted to facrifice a public benefit to
their own advantage. The bill, however, paffed, but more, as it feems, from a diffatisfac-
tion then prevailing between our court and Sweden, than from any patriotic motive. By the
permiffion granted to import both pig and bar

* POSTLETHWAYTE's *Commercial Dict.* Art. Naval
Stores.

iron

iron from America in Britifh veffels duty free, no inconfiderable advantages have been given to our foundries over thofe of other nations, * which added to the fuperior dexterity of our workmen, and the large capitals employed, have fecured us the market, even in countries whence we import the materials for this manufacture : it fhould ever be remembered, that if a duty upon raw materials be allowed in moft cafes to be prejudicial to the manufacture, it muft on iron perhaps be more fo than on any other commodity ; for being a principal article in naval ftores, it is of the higheft importance in fuch a country as this ; befide, as it may ferve in almoft all inftances for ballaft, &c. and is therefore of eafy tranfportation, even the freight on fuch a merchandife ought to be very moderate.

While the aforementioned Bills were depending in Parliament, a general alarm was fpread through the country, by reports of great wafte and deftruction of the woods in all thofe parts where Iron works were erected. POSTLE-THWAYTE, writing in the year 1759, fays, that "Where Cord-wood had before been fold at 5

*. The American Iron mines have an advantage over thofe of Ruffia in their proximity to the coaft ; for fome of the moft productive mines in Siberia are above 3000 miles from Peterfburgh.

"and

" and 6 fhillings the Cord, it then fold at
" upwards of 12 or 14, and in fome places was
" all confumed ; it is neceffary therefore," he
adds, "to preferve our timber from thefe con-
" fuming furnaces, left they at laft lay hold of
" our Oaks."* This is reported to have been
the cafe in Ireland alfo, where they have often
been obliged to procure even building timber
from Norway.‡ It is well known that the iron
works in Mendip-hills had long fince cleared
away all the oaks in that foreft, and that notwithftanding the fuccefsful adoption of Pit-coal
in fome of our moft extenfive works, woods are
ftill preferved in many places for the fupply of
the foundries.†

The ufe of wood in the iron works of France
is very general, owing to the great fcarcity of
coal in that country, and yet it is a remarkable
fact, that the provinces, where thofe manufac-

* *Commercial Intereft of Great Britain*, V. I. p. 151.
‡ The clamours of that day were increafed by the felf-
intereft of Wood, who made himfelf afterwards fo well
known in the Copper Coinage of Ireland. This man had
a leafe of all the mines on the Crown Lands of thirty-nine
counties, whofe furnaces were fupplied with pit-coal ; befide
iron work in various parts of the kingdom. ANDERSON's
Hift. of Commerce, V. II. p. 303.
† CAMPBELL's *Polit. Survey of Great Britain*, V.II. p. 43.

tories are eſtabliſhed, and eſpecially Burgundy, ſupply the Metropolis with more than two thirds of its fuel.‡

Great improvements have of late years been made in the proceſs of every branch in this valuable manufacture. The uſe of coak in England inſtead of charcoal, though ſome are of opinion that it debaſes the quality of the iron, has been found to anſwer for many of the larger works, and the application of ſteam to ſome of the moſt laborious operations, ſuch as the draining of coal, the ſupplying blaſts to the furnaces, the raiſing the forge hammer, promiſes ſtill further advantages.

The iron works in Colebroke Dale, are ſup-

‡ NECKER's *Adminiſtrat. of Finance,* &c. V. I. p. 255. At la Chauſade in the generality of Moulins, is an iron foundry, which 'during the late war furniſhed moſt of the extra anchors uſed in the Royal Navy of France. With half the labour there employed, the combined navy of France and Spain might have been ſupplied from ſuch foundries as thoſe of Colebroke Dale or Carron. At Moulins they excel in cutlery and in ſmall works, but in general Engliſh goods of this ſort have the preference even in the French markets; for it is a known fact, that Engliſh jewels and various toys and trinkets, *Bijouterie d'Angleterre,* are ſold *openly* and *avowedly* as ſuch at the *Palais Royal* at *Verſailles, Fontainbleau,* and even within the hearing of his Majeſty. TUCKER's Third Letter to Mr. NECKER, p. 45.

1

poſed

-pofed to be the moft extenfive in England,
employing upwards of one thoufand hands.
" The founders there earn from eight fhillings
" to ten fhillings and fix-pence a week, and
" boys of fourteen years old, feven fhillings, at
" drawing coal bafkets in the pits."* For pitcoal
is here principally ufed in making the bar iron.

The neighbouring hills fupply both in
fufficient quantities, and every ftep in the
procefs is performed on the fpot, from digging
the iron ore to the laft finifh of the manufacture.
Nothing can convey to a ftranger greater ideas
both of the ftock of raw materials, and the
ingenuity of the workman in this fingular fpot,
than the Bridge of caft iron, which now opens a
communication between two populous fides of
the Severn, and the waggon-ways paved with the
fame metal. The following picturefque remark
will give a fketch of the fcenery, and relieve the
neceffary drynefs of the fubject. " Colebroke
" Dale is a winding glen between two immenfe
" hills, which break into various forms, being all
" thickly covered and forming moft beautiful
" fheets of hanging woods. Indeed too beautiful
" to be much in unifon with that variety of

* Young's *Annals of Agric.* &c. V. IV. p. 167.

" horrors

" horrors which art has spread at the bottom.
" The noise of the forges, mills, &c. with all
" their vast machinery, the flames bursting
" from the furnaces, with the burning of the
" coal and the smoak of the lime kilns, are
" altogether horribly sublime, and would unite
" well with craggy and bare rocks like St.
" Vincents at Bristol." * The principal works
belong to Mr. Derby, Mr. Wilkinson, Mr.
Reynolds, and Messrs. Bancks and Onions;
the last of these are the proprietors of a
machine for boring cannon from the solid
cast; another of which is erected at Willey, by
Mr. Wilkinson.

It has been observed, that for many years
no cannon has been cast in that part called the
Dale Works, in which Quakers are employed;
" it being inconsistent with the principles of that
" peaceable sect, to make engines for the de-
" struction of their fellow creatures." ‡

The

---

* Young's *Annals*, &c. V. IV. p. 168. See also a more
particular account in the same volume, p. 343, &c. by
E. J. Harries, Esq. of Henwood.

‡ Ut sup. p. 348. The only articles in which our
iron manufactories seem to have suffered during the late
war, were Nails and Axes, but it is said the American
demand for these articles is now returning. Ut sup. p.
158.

Iron

The great irregularities and doubts in our Mine Laws contributed very much to retard the progress of improvement, in the preparation and working up of COPPER, though it was known to abound in many parts of the kingdom, till the present century. Since that time it has been brought to great perfection, and applied to almost as great a variety of uses as iron, especially in domestic utensils, for which it is peculiarly calculated by reason of its malleability, flexibility, elasticity, and ductility.* The principal copper mines in Europe are those near the Hartz and at Mifnia in Germany, in the Archbishopric of Saltzburg, in Bavaria, Wirtemburg, and Treves. In France, at Amiens, Abbeville, Rheims, Troyes, and Beauvais in many parts of Norway and Sweden, in the Dutchies of Parma and Placentia, near Brescia, and in Sicily.‡ Our own country produces

Iron imported according to the navigation-act, pays £2. 8. 6. a ton, and has a drawback on exportation of £2. 5. 2; in 1778, an additional 7s. 7d. If not imported according to the act, there is a duty of £2. 17. 10. a ton, and the drawback is £2. 14. 6. Iron wares manufactured not otherwise rated, or not prohibited, pay on importation 12s. 4d. and draw back on exportation 11s. 5d. The duty on iron wares manufactured in Ireland, is 14s. 3d. ⅓. a cwt. on importation.

* CAMPBELL's *Politic. Survey*, &c. V. II. p. 45.
‡ BEAUSOBRE, *Etude de la Politiq.* Tom. I. p. 151.

GREAT

great plenty of this metal, particularly in Cornwall, Staffordfhire, Somerfetfhire, and Cumber-
land. The mines of Cornwall, which produce
about a fifth part of the ore ufed in England, are
computed to afford to the value of £ 200,000*
annually; and in Anglefey, there is a mountain
which has a bed of this ore more than forty feet
in thicknefs, which fupplies annually between
fix and feven thoufand tons, and employs above
forty furnaces in fmelting it. Befide the pure
native Copper, there is a fpecies produced
by precipitation in vitriolic fprings in different
parts of Europe. Thofe of Wicklow in Ireland,
are very productive. It is faid that one ton of
iron bars laid on thefe fprings, produces a ton
and nineteen cwt. of Copper mud, and that
each ton of the mud when fmelted yields
fixteen cwt. of the pureft Copper, which fells
for £10 a ton more than the Copper which is
fluxed from the ore.‡ The Copper mills at
Namur

* *Philofophical Tranfactions*, V. XLVII. p. 502, V.
LXVIII. p. 94, and 101; WATSON's *Chemical Effays*, V. I.
ch. 6.

‡ BORLASE, *Nat. Hiftory of Cornwall*, p. 207. The fubordinate manufactories of brafs, verdigris, vitriol and pins
have fprung from the improvements made in the copper
branch. In the laft it is truly aftonifhing to confider the
many

Namur are perhaps the moſt extenſive in Europe, and it was there that the water-engine now in
common uſe, was firſt applied in the year 1695,
to put the ponderous machinery of theſe works
in motion.* If we may rely on the repreſen-
tations given, the ancients far exceeded us in
their manner of tempering and refining this
metal; at preſent the advantages of dexterity in
this branch, are not confined ſo particularly to
one country as to make it an object of commercial jealouſy. It is probable therefore that the
interchange between France and England for
commodities of Copper or Braſs, will be comparatively ſmall, and that they will continue to draw
their ſupplies chiefly from their own materials
and induſtry.‡

many ſubdiviſions of labour which are required to make
an article, ſo proverbially inſignificant. The engravers
and bell-founders alſo employ great quantities of this
metal.

* BEAUSOBRE, Etude de la Polit. T. II. p. 154.

‡ We are ſaid to export annually 2000 tons of vitriol.
Theſe works have lately much declined, by reaſon of the
home conſumption being ſupplied with the acid, as procured from the burning of ſulphur. WATSON's Chem.
Eſſays. V. I. p. 226.

HEMP.

HEMP and FLAX, confidered as the materials of various kinds of fabrics, are of the higheft confequence, and it may be obferved of them, that they place the connection between agriculture and manufacture in a ftronger light than any other produce of the foil. * There are few countries in Europe which do not grow them; thofe round the Baltic, particularly Ruffia, produce fuch great quantities, that they may be truly ftyled their ftaple commodities. † The Flax cultivated in Germany is intirely worked up at home, for the exportation of the raw materials is ftrictly prohibited; in confequence of this, the looms of that country fupply France with a great proportion of her linen goods, though of late years much attention has been paid to the cultivation of Flax in the provinces

* We read of two officers in the Roman empire, called *Procuratores Linificii*, who fuperintended the two great ftorehoufes at Ravenna and Vienne. From this circumftance much learned debate has been ftarted concerning the ftate of the cultivation and manufactories of Hemp and Flax among the ancients.

† It is calculated that Ruffia alone imports into England Hemp to the amount of 400,000 l. annually.

of

of Picardy, Brittany, Maine, Dauphiné, and Alſace. Flax alſo is plentifully produced in Flanders, eſpecially between Ghent and Cour- tray, where perhaps it is an object of more de- licate huſbandry than in any other part of Eu- rope. The conduct of the Flemiſh on this ar- ticle affords a good leſſon to monopoliſers of every claſs; for though linen and lace be the great manufactures of their country, they permit the free exportation of Flax on this principle, that it encourages production and improves cultiva- tion, and in the end renders the commodity both cheaper and better. The Flax in the province of Zealand is in high eſteem, and is uſed by the Dutch in the fabric of their finer linens, though it may be remarked, that weaving and whitening are in general the only parts of the whole proceſs performed to any great extent in Holland, and that moſt of the thread is ſpun in Germany and Pruſſia. The city of Bologna ſupplies Venice with both Hemp and Flax; and in Spain the provinces of Valencia, Grenada, and Murcia, furniſh the great manufactories of ſail-cloth and cordage eſtabliſhed at Port Real, and the linen fabrics in ſome of the neighbouring diſtricts. In this iſland, particularly in Scot- land, great attention has been paid to this branch of culture, though much diſpute has

K   ariſen

arifen on the expediency of carrying such a meafure to any length in South Britain.* It has been urged, that Hemp and Flax fo much exhauft and impoverifh the land, that it requires conftantly to be manured, and to lie fallow every third year at leaft; that the plants are exotics and degenerate in this country, fo that it is found neceffary to recruit them very frequently: to this it has been added, that to encourage their culture would be againft the intereft of fuch a country as England, becaufe it would moft probably operate to the difcouragement of the growth of *Wool*; moreover, that the fame effect would be produced here as is in France by the fubftitution of vineyards for farms; for as it is reckoned, that one acre of Flax will fet as many hands to work as twenty acres of Wool, it would in all probability too much reduce the price of land. The decreafe of the importation of Irifh Wool and Woollen Yarn into England about fifty years ago, it is afferted, was not owing, as generally furmifed, to its being run to France and other countries, but to the great increafe of the linen manufactures,

* See various Reports delivered to the Houfe in 1773, when Parliament was petitioned for a further aid to the linen manufactures.

4   efpecially

efpecially in Ulfter, which, for their fupply, had planted fuch quantities of Flax, that they had not fheep fufficient for their own markets, whereas not many years before they fupplied themfelves and the neighbouring provinces. *

Many of thefe objections, however, are difproved by experiment and obfervation. It has been found that there is much land in the north of England and in Scotland, which produces both Hemp and Flax as high and as ftrong as any imported from Riga; and that in fome other parts, they are cultivated in as fine a ftate as in the fouthern climates, infomuch, that Englifh Hemp has been known to fetch from 34 to 40s. the cwt. when what was brought from the Baltic ftood at 28 to 35s. and this cultivation is carried on in rich and deep foils without any fymptoms of impoverifhment or degeneration; on the contrary, we are told of a prodigious large field in the ifle of Axholm in Lincolnfhire, which though fowed with Hemp, has not been fallowed for many years, and always produces

---

* A Letter to a Member of Parliament in 1732, cited by ANDERSON, *Hift. Comm.* Vol. I. p. 340. It is faid that Flax, infufed in water, communicates a poifonous quality to it, which gave rife to Stat. 33 Hen. VIII. c. xvii. forbidding its being watered in any running ftream or common pond.

excellent

excellent crops; * this is also, in a great measure, the case at Spalding Moor in the East Riding of Yorkshire. † But be the fact as it may; surely there is room enough for very fair and extensive experiments of it, on some of the numerous moors and barren heaths of sand which disfigure this island.

The most reasonable objection seems to be the danger of diminishing the growth of Wool, by occupying much pasture land for these purposes, and consequently of sacrificing the interest of an ancient and valuable manufactory, to one which is by no means so productive or so natural to the people. Experience has now clearly proved, that the manufacture of *Linen* is very profitably established and carried on in countries where land and labour are cheap; on this account it has ever been the care of our Legislature to encourage it in Scotland and Ireland. By an Act passed in 1728, great advantages were granted to such as should introduce the Linen fabric into the Highlands, and since that time it has received occasional support by various premiums and bounties.

* GEE *on the Growth of Hemp and Flax.*

† CAMPBELL's *Politic. Survey,* &c. Vol. II. p. 89.

Their

Their good effects are sufficiently shewn by the following statements :

The value of the Linen stamped for sale in Scotland, was

From 1728 to 1733 - -	£. 662,938
From 1747 to 1752 - -	1,344,814
In 1754 alone - - -	506,816
In 1760 - - - -	522,153
In 1773 - - - - -	462,751
In 1774 - - - - -	492,055
In 1775 - - - - -	561,527
In 1777 - - - - -	710,633
In 1779 - - - - -	551,148
In 1780 - - - - -	622,187
In 1782 - - - - -	775,098
In 1783 - - - - -	866,983
And in 1784 - - - - -	932,617

Thus it appears, that though there was a sudden defect in 1773, it recovered and has almost doubled itself within the short space of these last ten years! The statutes made in the years 1696 and 1697,* " For encouraging the Linen manu-
" factories of Ireland, and for admitting the
" free importation of Flax and Hemp from that
" kingdom into England," were the means of

* 7 and 8 W. III.

carrying

carrying over many French refugees; and laid the foundation of her fabrics in Linen and Cambric; and two other Acts in 1703 and 1704, which extended this permiſſion in favour of Ireland to the Engliſh plantations in America *, ſtill further promoted their increaſe. Theſe privileges were not beſtowed inconſiderately; they were the reſult of mature and ſolid reaſoning on the natural and political ſituation of that iſland, and have fully anſwered their propoſed end. Some years previous to the paſſing the firſt of theſe Acts, Sir WILLIAM TEMPLE, among other reflections on the ſubject, obſerves, that " of all women, the Iriſh " were the apteſt and beſt calculated to ſpin " linen thread well; who, labouring little in " any kind with their hands, have their fingers " more ſupple and ſoft than others of as poor " condition amongſt us. This," he adds, " may certainly be improved into a great ma- " nufacture of Linen, ſo as to beat down the " trade of France and Holland, without croſſing " any intereſt of trade in England. Beſide " this, the ſoil and climate are peculiarly fit " for the growth of Flax and the whitening of " Linens." † This has been amply verified

* 3 and 4 Ann. c. viii.
† Miſcellanies, p. 13. Ed. 1681,

in

in the progrefs which the manufacture has made
during the prefent century. The particulars of
this matter have been fo frequently brought before the public of late years, that it would be
needlefs to enlarge upon them here. * The
following facts will be fufficient to fhew how
profitably fuch a branch of trade may be adopted, when circumftances like thofe in Ireland
or Scotland, concur to favour the cultivation of
its materials. It is calculated that an acre of
land will bear from 3 to 6 cwt. of flax, which
is worth 40s. a cwt. at the average therefore of
4 cwt. this will fet the produce of each acre at 8l.
The number of acres thus cultivated in Ireland
is computed at 13,000. So that the amount of
the whole produce is 104,000l. This produce
is raifed in its value eight times when in its
manufactured ftate, which brings it to 832,000l.
but it is faid, that a quantity equal to one
fifth of the raw materials grown in the country
is imported annually, this by adding 170,000l.
more, makes the whole annual amount of the
linen manufacture upwards of one million fterling. A ton of flax is fuppofed to employ

* Lord SHEFFIELD on the Irifh Trade. Arrangements with
Ireland confidered; with the Reports of the Linen Committees,
in 1773, and Vol. IX. Parliamentary Regifter.

annually

annually 40 perfons, and from the foregoing com-
putation it appears, that the quantity ufed is
about 3125 tons, fo that this manufactory employs upon the whole 125,000 hands. In
Scotland about 1540 tons are annually worked
up, which gives employment to 61,200 hands;
thus the linen manufactures in both countries,
may together be reckoned to employ 186,200
hands. From the fuperiority of wages it has
lately been feared, that the newly erected cotton works in many parts of Ireland may materi-
ally injure the linen branch; for a workman will
there earn from 13s. to 15s. a week, a lad of
13 years old 8s. or 9s. and at the fpinning-jenny
as much as 15s.—whereas at linen weaving the
worker of fine goods can earn no more than 8s. 6d.
and of coarfe goods no more than 6s. 3d. a week.
Girls alfo, who at flax fpinning get only 2s. or
3s. a week, will earn in the cotton works from
9s. to 11s. But the properties of flax appear
in a more ftriking point of view, when it is
confidered as the material of the *lace* manufacture. In Flanders where it has been, in this
branch, carried to its higheft perfection, they
reckon that one pound only, which is worth
from 4d. to 5d. will, when worked up, be raifed
to the value of 7000 florins, upwards of 600l.

which

which probably is as ſtrong an inſtance of the
lucrative effects of human ingenuity as can be
produced in the caſe of any other raw material
whatever. * And it has therefore been calculated, that if France were to exchange on equal
. terms, her wines for the lace of Bruſſels, ſhe
would give the produce of many thouſand acres
of wines for every ſingle acre of flax †

By 17 Geo. II. ch. xxx. the affixing counterfeit ſtamps to foreign linens imported, in
imitation of the ſtamps on Iriſh and Scotch
linens, and expoſing them to ſale, as alſo the
affixing counterfeit ſtamps to any linen manufactured in Great Britain or Ireland, and ex-

* A table exhibiting at one view the comparative price
of *firſt materials* with their proportionately *improved value*,
in every branch of manufacture and art, would be a curious and uſeful work.

† There is an excellent book on the ſubject of this chap-
ter, by Mr. MARCANDIER, of which there is an Engliſh
tranſlation in 1764. I quote the tranſlation from an opinion,
that even adepts in the French language will read works like
this, and all others which treat of agriculture, manufactures,
or finance, to the beſt advantage in good Engliſh tranſlations,
becauſe they muſt contain many terms of art and revenue,
and a variety of political idioms which it is difficult to com-
prehend ; for the ſame reaſon in matters of ſcience alſo it
is, in general, better to give extracts from foreign books in
our own language.

poſing

poſing the ſame to ſale, will incur the forfeiture of the goods and a penalty of 5l. for each piece. The different duties on the importation of this article are principally regulated by 10 Ann. c. xix. 12 Ann. c. ix. and 7 Geo. III. c. lviii. and lxxii.

W O O L.

During the 12th and 13th centuries the cloth manufactories of the Netherlands were the moſt flouriſhing in Europe, but being ill ſupplied with materials at home, they carried on an extenſive trade with this Iſland. To ſupply this great demand, a ſociety of merchants, called afterwards the *Wool Staplers*, combined for the purpoſe of collecting the Wool in various parts of the country to convey it to the ſea ports for exportation, and it appears that this branch of foreign traffic was for many years, not only permitted, but encouraged; indeed, it ſhould ſeem that, ſtrictly ſpeaking, the firſt *legal* prohibition occurs as late as the year 1660, by which forfeiture of the goods and ſhip, and a penalty of 20s. for every ſheep, and 3s. for every pound of wool exported, is incurred. * I am, neverthe-

* 12 Car. II. c. xxxii. § 3.

leſs,

lefs, aware that as far back as the reign of Edward III. temporary reftraints had been laid, and
that both James and Charles iffued proclama-
tions, and after them, the Long Parliament in-
terpofed its authority with this view;* it
fhould alfo be remembered, that though a fubfidy on the raw material was very common in
earlier times, yet the firft regular grant on the
manufacture occurs in 21 Edward III. " This,"
fays HALE, " was founded on reafon and equity, for as the King had a cuftom of inheritance
fettled in him of Wools exported, and much of
our Wool now began to be draped into cloth
and thus exported, it was thought fit, that he
fhould have his proportionate benefit of this
commodity exported in *manufacture* as well as in
fpecie."✝ It was in this king's reign alfo, that the
woollen manufactory firft gained a rooted eftablifhment in this country. RYMER has preferved
a letter of protection, fent by Edward in the
year 1331, to a manufacturer in Flanders, to
invite him and his family to fettle in England; ‡
and

---

* RYMER's *Fœdera*, Tom. IV. fol. 744. Tom. XIX.
fol. 155.

✝ HARGRAVE's *Law Tracts*, cap. xxvi. and cap. ix. of
the third part of HALE's MS.

‡ *Fœdera*, Tom. IV. fol. 496. For various regulations
of Ed. III. in this article, fee alfo Tom. IV. fol. 702.

and many other families we are informed followed their example. DE WITT, fpeaking of
this event, obferves, that before the removal
of the weaving trade to England, the Englifh
were little better than fhepherds; but this ftep
was the foundation of her commercial glory,
and the ruin of the Netherlands." *

It was then that our anceftors began to feel
their real intereft, and difcovered that whilft
men, women, and children were bufied in working up the *fleece*, they were alfo fed with the
mutton. Then our people multiplied, they acquired wealth and power, and left the Nobles
of the land fhould forget the fleece, they were
feated upon *woolfacks* in the Senate Houfe. †
Notwithftanding the increafed demand for home
confumption, which muft neceffarily have followed this event, we find that the duties from
the foreign fale of raw wool amounted, even
then, to 250,000l. annually. ‡   This ftrongly

720. 723. 736. 744. 751. 757. Very coarfe cloths were made
in England before this time, and it was not till the reign of
Elizabeth that the manufactory of the very fine fort was
eftablifhed.

* *Intereft of Holland*, p. 27.

† MOORE's *Confiderations on the exorbitant Price of Provifions*, p. 42.

‡ *Memoirs of Wool*, V. I. p 82.

illuftrates

illuſtrates an obſervation, that the market for this article in the rude beginnings of improvement is very ſeldom confined to the country which produces it; becauſe being eaſily tranſported without any preparation, and affording materials for many manufactures, the induſtry of other countries may occaſion a demand much beyond that of its native country. * The unjuſtifiable ſeverity of our ſtatutes againſt the exporters of Wool has been compared to the ſpirit of *Draco*'s laws. The 8th Eliz. c. iii. is a diſgrace to any penal code; it is however virtually repealed by the ſtatute of Charles above-mentioned, which is itſelf alſo, with reſpect to the penalty, expreſsly repealed. But cruel and impolitic as ſuch prohibitions may now appear, they might at that time have been neceſſary; for before ſuch manufactories have arrived at a tolerable degree of perfection, fiſcal law requires to be ſanctioned with heavy penalties, in order to prevent the unprofitable exchange of fabrics, in return for raw materials.

At the cloſe of the laſt century the practice of *owling*, as it was termed, that is ſmuggling the Wools of England and Ireland into France, was a ſubject of heavy complaint. †

* *Wealth of Nations*, B. I. c. ii.

† ANDERSON'*s Hiſtory of Commerce*, Vol. II. p. 126.

The

The unlimited extent of our market-rendered the conduct of our own ftaplers inexcufable in this refpect, and a very fit object of parliamentary control : but, after the reftrictive claufes in 7 and 8 W. III. c. 28, it might naturally be expected, that fuch a ftep would be taken by the fifter kingdom. An attempt to monopolize a branch of trade, by paffing laws to limit its price in the market, is in effect little elfe than to beftow bounties upon fmuggling. Statutes may pafs and penalties may be inflicted, but it will never prevent materials of general demand from finding their way clandeftinely to the moft advantageous purchafer. * This the Venetians experienced in the 16th century, when they aimed at a monopoly of the raw filks of Cyprus at a ftated price, and actually appointed officers to watch and regifter the exportations of that ifland, yet with all their care, the inhabitants contrived to fmuggle immenfe quantities of this article to Marfeilles, and various other French and Italian ports in the Mediterranean. † In the fame manner and for the fame reafons the Irifh

* 12 and 22 Geo. II. in a great meafure remedied this evil, and it was further relieved in 1778, and again in 1780 and 1781.

† Mauroceni, *Hiftoria Venetiæ*, p. 543, Edit. Argentor. 1692.

woollen

woollen trade found its way into France. It was carried to such an alarming length about thirty years ago, that it became a matter of very serious consideration. The advantages which France must derive by such a contraband trade are obvious, when it is understood that for many purposes, her own wool is too coarse and short in the staple, but being mixed in the proportion of two packs to one of Irish or English wool, it can be worked up very profitably into what is termed the best second cloths, which are those in most general use. It was then and has since been the received opinion, that no other mode of preventing this grievance, could be more beneficially adopted, than that of permitting the Irish to send their manufactured woollens to England, under a duty at importation, to be drawn back on exportation to foreign countries. * A proposed Bill " for preventing the smuggling of Wool," &c. has lately been the cause of general meetings in some of our coast counties, the results of

* The effect of the woollen trade of France on our market, at the beginning of this century, is exemplified by the following fact: When the plague raged at Marseilles, the demand of foreign countries for woollen goods were so large, that wool of both England and Ireland were insufficient to supply them. Jos. GEE, *Trade and Navigation*, &c. p. 67. POSTLETHWAYTE's *Commercial Interest*, &c. V. I. p. 363.

which

which are already before the public. The spirited resolutions of the meeting held in the county of Suffex, called forth a letter from Mr. JOHN ANSTIE, who maintains that the present laws are so defective as to want a thorough revision, and, that, although it is difficult in this branch so to regulate them, that they shall not impose restrictions on particular persons, yet he trusts, that such considerations will have no weight in decisions of Parliament *

I shall now proceed to state a few particulars respecting this valuable material and its manufacture. In point of quality the Wool of Spain claims the first rank, and of this what is called the *Escurial Fleece* is the finest and the dearest. It sells sometimes on the spot for 6 livres, about 5s. a pound, which is more by two livres than the average price of Spanish wool in France. The wools of Castille and Arragon, and the black wool of Saragossa, are also in high estimation. When next to Spain, England is allowed

* See *A Letter to the Land Owners, Wool Growers, &c. in the County of Suffex*, dated Devises, Nov. 21, in the " Morning Chronicle," It was upon the result of an examination of Mr. ANSTIE and Mr. AFFLECK before a Committee of the House of Commons, and in consequence of their report, that leave was given to bring in the Bill.

to produce this article in the greateſt perfection, it muſt not be underſtood in too general
a ſenſe; for there is ſcarcely any thing more
variable in its price and quality than Engliſh
wool. The fleeces in the neighbourhood of
Roſs, in Herefordſhire, are extremely fine,
and have been known to ſell as high as
2s. 4d. the pound, though at other times they
fetch as low a price as 1s.—they were lately
at 16d. the pound. The South Downs produce wool from 9d. to 1s. 10d. the pound; this
is alſo the average price of ſome of the fine
foreſt wools, which when mixed with the Spaniſh, ſerve to make the ſecond priced fine
cloths. The wool near Bridgnorth and about
the Wrekin in Shropſhire, is in general bought
at 1s. 6d. the pound, and this is uſually the
price of Lemſter wool. In many parts of Lin-
colnſhire it is at 6d. in the Weſt Country at
4½d. and on Romney Marſh, it has been
known to ſell at 3d the pound. In ſhort, it
would appear, upon a more particular inveſtiga-
tion, that between the extremes of Herefordſhire and Kent, there are all the various prices
from 2s. 6d. to 3d. in the pound. A univer-
ſal average through the kingdom therefore, as
it is in many other caſes, muſt be in this inſtance deceitful and unſatisfactory, and it has

L   accordingly

accordingly been ftated to be from 8d. to 1s.
the pound. One obfervation, however, may
arife from fuch a ftatement, namely, that the
average price, fince the reign of Ed. III.
has fallen, for wool was then fold at about
2l. 16s. a pack, or 2½d. a pound : this has
happened becaufe our prohibitions on exportation, our grants of importation, duty free, from
Spain, and our monopoly of the exportation
from Ireland, all confpired to enlarge the
market ftock, notwithftanding the great increafe of demand from the improved ftate of
fociety, and the extention of our manufactories. *   As the quality of an article, in a great
meafure, regulates its price, this alfo is found
to be proportionally various in different parts of
the kingdom. †   It is unneceffary to enter
largely into this matter. I fhall only obferve,
that the wool of Herefordfhire and Shropfhire,

---

* Smith's *Memoirs of Wool*, V. I. p. 6. 17. 44. V. II.
p. 9. 54. 176. 182. Prohibited exportation has, in Portugal, a fimilar influence on the price of its gold and
filver. N. B. The price of wool in very early times is
eafily afcertained, becaufe it was common to pay the King's
fubfidy in this article. The average price in Ireland has
lately been from 9d. to 14d.

† Wool in quantity alfo is remarkably uncertain, for it
has been known, that 20 fleeces of fine wool have fcarcely
weighed more than one of a larger fort.

and

and fome of the heath wools are preferred to mix with the Spanifh, for the beft fuperfine cloth, and that it is principally from the wool of Lincolnfhire, Nottingham, Northamptonfhire, and parts of Kent, that our worfted goods are manufactured. That of Lincolnfhire, though coarfer than the Kentifh wool, being longer in the ftaple, is in great requeft for the Norwich manufactories, and it has been thought that both of them might be fuccefsfully fubftituted in the room of Spanifh wool for making the chain of the finer cloths; a matter which furely deferves fome attention, when it is remembered how much the quantity of fine wool is diminifhed lately in Shropfhire and many other parts of England, from the introduction of a large breed of fheep, by means of inclofures and artificial graffes. The Scotch wool, it is imagined, if it were not greafed and tarred to preferve the animal, would, in many parts, equal the finenefs of our Herefordfhire fleeces. Spanifh wool is purchafed in England from 2s. 3d. to 3s. 9d. a pound, though the late average has been from 3s. 7d. to 4s. It is faid that $\frac{9}{10}$ of what is ufed is of the quality from 3s. 2d. to 3s. 9d. a pound, and that a yard of broad cloth requires two pounds and a half of

this

this wool. France has never excelled in the growth of this article, but has always depended upon foreigners, for the materials of her beft woollen manufactures. By the Family Compact, fhe imports the wool of Spain, free of all duty for ever, and it is to be feared that fhe is indebted to the flocks of Lincolnfhire and Kent for many of thofe long combing fleeces, which are worked up at Amiens, Abbeville, and the various manufactories of Normandy, and Bretagne, * which fhe receives principally through the Low Countries.

The province of Berry, famous for a peculiar kind of Cloth which goes by its name, is faid to be fupplied with wool from fheep of its own growth, and we are lately told that M. D'AUBENTON, near Montbard, in Burgundy, has a breed of fheep whofe wool is fo fine as to be fold at five livres the pound. This gentleman is one of the principal promoters of a fpirit which is now gone forth in France, for encouraging and improving the

* Amiens and Abbeville, in Picardy; Darnetal, Fefchamp, Caen, St. Lo, Alençon, Rennes, Bourg, and St. Brieux, in Bretagne, are the chief woollen manufactories, though there are many others of note in thofe provinces: they are, for the moft part, employed on ratteens, ferges, and fine cloths, fome of which they profefs to make entirely of Spanifh wool.

growth

growth of Wool : He is the author of a work
called *Inftruction pour les Bergers et pour les Pro-
prietaires de Troupeaux*, which, though not fo
extenfive as M. CARLIER's *Traité des Bétes à
Laine*, from its form and the fimplicity of its
ftyle, is better calculated to have its intended
effect. Thefe are mentioned, as good antidotes
to any defpondencies which may arife upon
hearing of fuch national exertions among our
neighbours, for they prove that their countrymen are at prefent fo very far behind us in the
cultivation of fheep, and labour againft fuch a
variety of natural and political obftructions, that
there can be little room for jealoufy on our part.
Much has been faid of the lownefs of wages
and the cheapnefs of materials in this branch of
French manufacture, yet it is very demonftrable,
that both their very fine cloths and their coarfe
woollens are as dear as in England. The beft
cloths of Sedan, Louviers, and Abbeville, fell
at twenty fhillings the Englifh yard, and they
are generally thought to be of a flighter texture
and lefs durable than our fuperfines. At
Auxerre, Samur Macon, Grenoble, Vienne,
Arles, and many towns in the province of
Orleans, coarfe woollen Serges are for their
quality, found to be higher priced than the fame

L 3   articles

articles are with us : Their fecond cloths alfo, which do not excel ours of twelve fhillings the yard, either in the texture or the dreffing, are fold at Vervins, Fontaine, Chalons, and other parts of Champagne, and about Poictiers, from fifteen to fixteen livres four fols the yard : At Romantin indeed, in the generality of Orleans, there is a manufactory of white cloths, made with equal proportions of Spanifh and Berry wool, which is in high eftimation, and from certain local advantages, fends out its goods better finifhed, and at a more reafonable price. Of the preference given to our woollens before thofe of France, LORD SHEFFIELD has related a curious inftance. " In the late war, when " France granted a fum of money to Congrefs, " for cloathing the American troops, Mr. " Laurens, jun. was employed to provide it; " but inftead of laying out the money in France, " he went to Holland, and bought Englifh " cloths, and fent them to America. The " French Minifter complained, but Mr. L. " juftified himfelf by faying it was his duty to " do the beft he could with the money, and that " the Englifh cloths of equal price with the " French, were much better."*

* *Obfervations on the Commerce of the American States*, p. 11.

In

In the preparation of our woollen cloths, and the manner of offering them to the market, the procefs in the north of England and in the weft, is remarkably different. It may readily be conceived by a little reflection, how, not only the price of the commodity and its propofed quality, but the induftry alfo, and even the morals of the workmen may be affected by this circumftance. Let us compare with fuch a view the ftate of the two manufactories; though it muft be confeffed, that by the general affimilation of manners and cuftoms, which has fpread of late years into the remoteft provinces, and among all ranks of life, the lines of contraft are gradually growing fainter.

In many parts of Yorkfhire, the woollen manufactory is carried on by fmall farmers and freeholders, who both buy and grow wool, and whofe wives, daughters, and fervants fpin it in the long winter evenings, and at fuch times as they are not employed in their farms and dairies; the mafter of the family either fells this produce in the yarn market, or has it wove up himfelf. It is then milled, cleanfed, and brought to market, but when fold there, he can be paid for no greater number of yards than the cloth will meafure after having been well foaked in water. Thus all frauds in ftretching, tentering, &c. are

effectually

effectually · prevented. The persons who buy this cloth, generally act upon commiffion, at a very low rate; and afterwards get the cloth dyed, dreffed, and finifhed. The whole in this manner paffes through various hands independent of each other, and being thus independent, they are all rivals, and are animated with the fame defire of bringing their goods to market upon the cheapeft terms, and of excelling each other. Their journeymen likewife are little removed from the degree and condition of their mafters, and know that the induftry and frugality of a few years will enable them to fet up for themfelves. Thus they are generally moral, fober, and diligent, the goods are well made and cheap; and a riot or a mob fcarcely known amongft them. In the Weft, this whole bufinefs is carried on by a very different procefs, and the effects are accordingly oppofite. Here one perfon with a great ftock and large credit, buys the wool, is mafter of the whole manufactory from the firft ftage to the laft, and employs perhaps a thoufand perfons under him; thefe, many of them, work together in the fame fhop, confequently have opportunities to corrupt each other, and to cabal againft their mafters. They have little hope of advancing themfelves by their induftry, and therefore think it no crime to

get

get as much wages as poffible, and too often
reconcile their confciences to frauds on their
mafter's property. It is needlefs to point out
the other ill effects of fuch management; they
have frequently made themfelves fufficiently
notorious in riots and infurrections.* I fhall not
enter into any particulars on either of thefe
manufactories, but cannot forbear adding one
remark more before I quit the fubject.

In a *Letter* figned A WOOLLEN DRAPER, we
are told of above *five hundred* clothing towns in
France, upon the authority of a Lift, publifhed
about fix and twenty years ago.‡ Now admitting this to bear as ftrongly on the point as
poffible, if the writer really *be* that *Woollen
Draper* which he would wifh to *feem*, he cannot
be ignorant of the infufficiency of fuch a ftatement alone, to eftablifh any eftimate. But I
can take upon me to affert on my own obfervation and inquiries, that from fome of the towns
enumerated in his lift, the fcanty trade carried
on in the year 1760, has totally vanifhed, that in

* As I never remember to have met with a clearer account of this well-known diftinction between our northern
and weftern Clothiers, I did not fcruple to adopt it almoft
in the very words of a Pamphlet now become fcarce, called
Inftructions for Travellers, by Dr. TUCKER.

‡ P. 14, and the Lift annexed to the *Letter*.

fome

fome others, particularly in Champagne and Soiffons, the bufinefs is conducted on a very contracted fcale, for the moft part in a few private houfes, and that in many places which formerly were famous for their fine cloths, the looms are now principally employed in the working of Serges, Etamines, and light Druggets. It muft at the fame time be confeffed that new manufactories both of fine and coarfe Woollens have been erected in that kingdom, and that fome old ones have been extended; but numbers alone are an inadequate teft in this matter; it may admit of a doubt, if we except Langue-doc, whether the broad looms of Gloucefterfhire and Wiltfhire do not annually fend to market, almoft as large a quantity of the very beft cloths, as all the provinces of France. How long this may continue to be the cafe, is another queftion. On this fcore, the WOOLLEN DRAPER merits every commendation for the zealous and fenfible manner in which he ftands forth to call the atten-tion of his countrymen and fellow traders to a point fo clofely connected with their future com-mercial welfare. To a perfon whofe inquiries have never been directed to the fubject, it is not eafy to explain how wide an influence the ftate of our Woollen trade has on national profperity. Falling on many other branches of manufacture,

an

an injury may be comparatively partial, and
though perhaps feverely felt for a time, by
that clafs of artificers whofe ftock and fkill are
engaged, will not occafion much diftrefs, beyond
a certain neighbourhood and a particular rank
of men : But *the Manufacture of the Fleece* is
accompanied by fuch a train of connections and
dependencies through which it both communicates and receives fupport, difperfes employment and wealth among fuch a variety of
departments, and is fo undiftinguifhably united
with our Landed Property, that it neceffarily
involves in its fate, the interefts of the whole
community, from the Yeomanry to the Throne.
On the difcuffion therefore of an article fo extenfive and important in its confequences, we
have no reafon to doubt that the wifdom of the
Legiflature will be difpaffionately exerted :
That on one hand they will not fuffer the
prejudices of falfe patriotifm or the low jealoufies
of trade to obftruct the meafure, if it appear to
be expedient, merely becaufe it may confer
equal and reciprocal advantages ; nor on the
other, be prevailed upon by fpecious arguments
and interefted declamation, to run any rifk of
facrificing the produce perhaps of more than
half the looms in the Weft of England, to the

unneceffary

unneceſſary Porcélains of Worceſter, or the ornamental Toys of Sheffield, Saliſbury, and Birmingham.

GENERAL REFLECTIONS.

There is ſcarcely any point in POLITICAL ŒCONOMY which has been ſo variouſly diſcuſſed, as *the effect of the price of labour on Commercial Competition.** It ſhould be obſerved, that the queſtion of high and low wages is not to be determined merely by the pay of the workmen, but by the proportion which ſuch wages bear to the prices of all other articles, either native or foreign, and by comparing the manufactured product alſo of different countries, with a view to diſcover at what average price the ſame goods can be equally well made in each. By ſuch a mode of inquiry it will in general be found, that labour in a country of low wages is comparatively dearer, than where wages are high, and that conſequently in moſt caſes the rich country will be able to underſell the poor one, becauſe its goods will more than compenſate by their quality for any exceſs of price. It cannot be

* TUCKER's *Four Tracts*, Tract. I.—SMITH's *Wealth of Nations*, B. I. c. viii. Edit. 1786.

doubted,

doubted, that as " the liberal reward of labour
" is the neceſſary effect, ſo is it the natural
" ſymptom of increaſing wealth ;" for when the
productive powers of labour and ingenuity are
thus excited, induſtry muſt in all its departments
become more refined, as well as more dextrous
and active in its exertions. In a manufactory
where the different proceſſes are diſtributed to
different workmen, each will in his diſtinct
branch be more expert than if he were under the
neceſſity of undertaking many different branches
at once in order to gain ſubſiſtence. Such
dexterity begets competition, and this neceſſa-
rily reduces the price; " whereas in the country
" of low wages, it is in the power of one wealthy
" man, to monopolize the trade, and to ſet
" what price he chuſes on his goods."* That
the low price of labour will not command a
market, may be ſhewn by the following in-
ſtances : When the iron of Sweden arrives in
England, it has paid duties of export, import,
and the expence of freight ; to this muſt be
added the coſts of carriage to and from the
places of manufacture, the price of the labour
there beſtowed upon it, and the duty to which
it is liable on its return home under this new

* *Four Tracts*, p. 34.

form ;

form ; yet with all this accumulated charge upon
it, we are able to underfell the Swedes themfelves in their own market ; and every attempt
on their part at competition has proved hitherto
ineffectual. It is exactly the fame cafe with the
Bay Yarn of Ireland, which, notwithftanding all the charges of importation, conveyance
and manufacture, is worked up here and
returned cheaper to the Irifh market, than
if it had been manufactured at home. It is not,
as fome have lately afferted, the higher price of
our labour which has given the French an advantage over us in the Levant and Portugal
trades, but rather the indifference of our manufactures, and their unwillingnefs to accommodate
their fabrics to the tafte of thofe markets, in
which, by reafon of the climate, cheap cloths of
a flight texture will ever be preferred to fuch as
are more durable. After all, it may be doubted
whether it would be worth while for our
clothiers to attempt the recovery of this trade,
at the rifk of facrificing a better ; for every
loom employed in the weaving of Druggets,
muft occupy materials and labour which might
be more profitably applied in the working of
broad cloths ; add to this, that the fame competition which would be ferviceable in higher
branches, by rendering the goods cheap, muft
here

here be prejudicial, becaufe the original low
price of the commodity, would fink the neceffary
reduction of profits beneath the merchant's confideration. An effort made at Penryn, in Cornwall, about 30 years ago, proved unfuccefsful
for want of proper encouragement, and almoft
ruined the patriotic projector.* Ireland indeed
by being admitted to the advantages of the
Methuen-Treaty, might in time, perhaps, be
enabled to fupplant France in the Drugget
trade. But the circumftance of being underfold
is not the only ground of apprehenfion for the
fafety of trade, with thofe who draw their arguments from a comparifon between the value of
labour in different countries. The danger of
emigration has been largely infifted upon, and
fears have been fuggefted that manufactories
will be transferred from a dear country, to one
where the means of fubfiftence are cheap. It
would be lofs of time to fhew the fallacy of fuch
a fuppofition, and the abfurdity of conceiving

* I will not fuppofe fo little virtue to be in that part of
England, as the Author of *Propofitions for improving the
Manufactories, &c. of Great Britain*, in 1763, would infi-
nuate, when he fays, "this gentleman was almoft ruined,
" becaufe he thought it his duty to vote againft the prefent
" reprefentatives of the borough of Penryn, at the laft
" general election." p. 32.

4   that

that artificers of any clafs would voluntarily exchange high wages for low, or, in other words, would . quit good provifions and comfortable habitations, for meagre fare and wretched hovels. In fact, the high price even of the neceffaries of life, has feldom been injurious to the progrefs of induftry, nay in fome inftances it has been the means of calling forth new and fuccefsful exertions of labour and fkill, and has led to very important difcoveries in Arts and Manufactories. It was when the Piedmontefe were oppreffed by the taxes and exactions of the SFORZAS, who for fome years perfifted in heavy affeffments of their harvefts, and their markets, that they firft carried their fabrics of filk to a degree of refinement and expedition, by the introduction of mechanifm into fome parts of the procefs, that no European country was able to enter into competition with them.* It is not difficult in

fhort

* MURATORI, Differt. VII. Tom. III. It is through them we are indebted to this circumftance, perhaps, for LOMBE's ftupendous Machine, on the river Derwent, near Derby. He procured a model of it in Piedmont, by working under the difguife of a common Weaver.—By 5 GEO. II. c. viii. SIR. T. LOMBE obtained 14,000l. as a reward for this fervice to the Silk Manufactory. The Machine contains 26,586 wheels, and 97,746 movements, which

work

fhort to conceive, that, in a ftate where the balance between the prices of labour and of wages is left to regulate itfelf, and is never made the objeƈt of civil policy, the rate of common fubfiftence and of the conveniences of life may be fo low as to prevent any improvement in manufaƈtures, if not entirely to exclude them. In opulent countries fuperior fkill may often countervail the effeƈt of high wages. This is obvious in all thofe articles where labour and materials are the leaft part of the value, and may be exemplified in moft of the articles in the warehoufes of Manchefter and Birmingham.

A want of tafte and variety in their fabrics was formerly the general complaint againft our Englifh manufaƈturers, and they were on that account frequently fupplanted by their neigh-bouring rivals, the French, whofe accommodating invention was continually devifing new forms and patterns of goods, and ftudying textures fuited to the tafte and climate of their various cuftomers ; but of late years a total revolution has been effeƈted in our manufac-

work 73,726 yards of organzine filk thread every time the water wheel goes round, which it does thrice in a minute. Its ereƈtion in this country was confidered as fuch an injury to Piedmont, that an Italian artift, it is faid, was fent over to England to affaffinate the proprietor.

turcs ;

tures; for while in fome of them, men of fcientific and liberal minds have, by a feries of well-conducted experiments, produced new forms and combinations of materials, others have beftowed upon them fuch variety, ftrength, and beauty of workmanfhip, that they are diftinguifhed by a decided preference in almoft every market. This is the cafe in Switzerland, with refpect to our cottons, woollens, and various articles of houfehold furniture, our finer works in iron and fteel, the claffical productions of our *Englifh Etruria,* and the long catalogue of toys and trinkets, notwithftanding the vicinity of France, and the boafted cheapnefs of her labour.* It is ftill more pointedly the cafe in America, for when that country had contracted a debt of four million fterling, to the merchants of this ifland, for accumulated ftores of Britifh manufacture, they attempted to feek fupplies in their own induftry, and in the trade of France and Holland; but what has been the confequence? after many fruitlefs attempts to fuperfede the ufe of our manufactures, they have at laft chofen to become our cuftomers again, becaufe, as their merchants confefs, our fabrics are better and cheaper than thofe of other coun-

* Tucker's *Third Letter to Necker,* p. 39, 41.

4

tries, and this they think it for their advantage to do, though (as it hath been obferved) " at " an expence of 40 per cent. at leaft dearer than " they might have done had they continued " their allegiance;" it appears alfo that even in the late war, fuch was the preference given to our cotton manufactures, that the Manchefter traders could have found employment for many thoufand additional hands.*

Examples might eafily be multiplied, if it were neceffary, to fhew the fallacy of conclufions, in favour of the manufacturing intereft, drawn from the low price of provifions and labour. Our fifter kingdom would furnifh many; for there, notwithftanding the patriotic bounties of the Dublin Society, and a great variety of parliamentary aids, Britifh manufactures of almoft every fort, under the difadvantages of Freight, Duties, Land Carriage, and Commiffion, are able fuccefsfully to compete with Irifh goods in their own market. The more labour and ingenuity is exerted in any manufacture, the ftronger will thefe principles be found to operate on the competition in favour of the rich country. Timber and metals

* Lord SHEFFIELD's *Commerce of the American States*, p. 28.

may

may be procured more readily, and purchafed cheaper in the forefts of Norway, and at the mines of Siberia; but trace thefe materials through the whole progrefs of their fabrication in different countries, the moft advantageous market will be found among people who are rich and flourifhing, whofe artificers more than compenfate by their dexterity and expedition for the advanced price of their wages. The tedious and aukward procefs of undivided labour, a neceffary effect of flender capitals, muft fhrink from fuch a competition, nor prefume to oppofe any negative or partial benefits to be derived from poverty, to that fpirit of enterprize, that habitual induftry and fkill, which are in opulent kingdoms excited, cherifhed and improved, by the animating influence of large Demand, the fecurity of Stock, the unimpeded circulation of Capital, high Credit, and extenfive Correfpondence.

It is in fuch countries, that the happy effects of liberal reward are exemplified in a variety of inventions, conducive to the real comforts of life, and in works of ingenuity and tafte, which innocently add to the elegancies of fociety: even exotic manufactures, under fuch circumftances, will be tranfplanted and carried to maturity, with compa-

ratively

ratively lefs care and expence than foreign vegeta-
bles : another country may indeed, in fome articles, enjoy certain local and natural advantages,
againſt which competition would be impolitic,
and in fuch a cafe there is no doubt, greater
benefit would arife by becoming her cuſtomer,
than by waſting capitals in extravagant projects,
which might be very productively employed in
native manufactories. " It would be an unreafonable law to prohibit the importation of all
foreign wines, merely to encourage the making
of Claret and Burgundy in Britain," * and in
this inftance it might be for the intereſt of a
country to be underfold by foreigners in her
own market ; but I cannot agree to make fo general an application of this rule as fome writers
have done, or to fubfcribe to that unqualified
pofition, that whenever a manufactory cannot
ſtand the teſt of competition, the fooner it is
aboliſhed the better : great allowances ſhould
be made for the periodical derangements to
which all artificial fyſtems are liable, nor are
our fabricks of filk and cotton to be immediately aboliſhed, though they may not enjoy
that uninterrupted train of fuccefs, which ufually attends a manufacture fupplied with native

Wealth of Nations, B. IV. ch. ii.

materials.

materials. Had such policy been pursued, the wealth of *Coventry* had never been added to the general stock, * nor *Paisley* have supplanted the silks of *Spitalfields*, or supplied (as is known to be the case with that manufacture) most countries in Europe with its gauzes. The materials of the cotton manufactory are entirely of foreign growth, but being estimated, as every manufactory ought to be, in proportion to its power of improving such materials, and according to its demand of skill and labour, there are few which can claim a preference. It may be doubted, whether, in any branch of business, larger capitals are at present embarked than in this; yet it is not many years since doubts were entertained, how far it might be expedient to encourage a manufacture which seemed so likely to intrench upon the interests of our woollen trade ; † and the same bad policy

* The average annual amount of ribbands manufactured at that place is about 500,000l. KEYSLER in his Travels, in the year 1730, having spoken of the difficulties with which the silk manufacture of this country long struggled, adds, " but now in Italy itself the silks of England are most esteemed, and bear a greater price than those of Italy ; so that at Naples when a tradesman would highly recommend his goods, he protests they are right English." *Collection of Travels*, V. II. p. 276.

† *An Examination of the Commercial Principles of the late Negotiation*, 8vo. p. 137. 1762.

which

which has oppreffed many other branches, was
foon after exerted upon this, by fubjecting its
materials to a duty on importation. Nothing
but that fuperiority of fkill and capital, which
characterizes the trade of England, and ena-
bles it to maintain the market under many difadvantages, could have fupported the fabricks
of Manchefter thus taxed, againft the fpirited
exertions of the Rouen manufactory, conducted
by an Englifh artift, * and affifted in its capital
by large periodical fupplies from Government.
That the cotton manufactory has, in fome
meafure, been injurious to the woollen branch
cannot be difputed, but whether this ought to
be confidered as a *univerfal* injury, may admit
of doubt ; fuch an inference cannot furely be
drawn from any influence it has had in the
neighbourhood of its fettlement, either in England or Ireland, nor from its general effects on
our national wealth and population. † But as a
proof

* Mr HOLKER. Two of ARKWRIGHT's Mills are now
erected in the neighbourhood of Rouen. The judicious
bounty of OUR KING, to the newly erected Cottonworks, at Eton, is worthy of grateful remembrance.

† It is computed, that in Lancafhire, Chefhire, Derby-
fhire, Nottinghamfhire, and Leicefterfhire, above 500,000
perfons,

proof to how great a length the contracted jealoufies of trade may be carried, we have heard even the Linen manufactory exclaimed againft, as an exotic. About fifteen years ago, when a bill was propofed for its encouragement, the zealous advocates for the woollen trade were not content to oppofe the Bill on what might have been admitted as tenable ground, but attempted to convert a *political objection* to the expediency of the meafure into a *phyfical impediment* to the production of the materials neceffary in this fabric. If it be allowed to argue from our home confumption, we may queftion whether under proper regulations our Linen manufactory might not be rendered as productive as our Cotton; for it has been computed, that we afford at prefent a market to Ireland in this article, to the amount of one million fterling annually, and that although four fifths of this

perfons, including women and children, are employed in the cotton branch. In Ireland, befide the eftablifhments near Dublin, there are now large Cottonworks in the county of Kildare. Their rapid progrefs may be inferred from this circumftance, that a folitary cottage on the Bog of Allen, in the year 1780, is now converted into a flourifhing town. SHEFFIELD's *State of Ireland*, p. 197.

importation

importation be for home confumption, we ftill find employment for our own manufactories to an equal if not a greater amount.* Men who fuffer themfelves to be thus governed by the felfifh and illiberal principle of monopoly, will find perpetual occafion for jealoufy and alarm, fince every benefit conferred upon another branch of trade, muft feem to operate as an injury to their own. Each clafs has fome partial view to gratify for its profeffional advantage; that which will fuit the Manchefter trader may prejudice the merchant of Leeds, and the gratification of both thefe will raife an outcry in Birmingham, and Staffordfhire. But it is not the flourifhing or the declining ftate of any particular manufacture, that neceffarily implies general ruin, or that ought to impede a meafure falutary to the reft. Minds truly patriotic are fwayed in their operations by nobler motives, and aim at objects more extenfive and important than the gratification of private intereft.

It fhould be the object of a commercial country to obferve a fcrupulous impartiality in the extenfion of its care to every ufeful branch

* A report of the late board of trade, relative to the linen manufacture in July, 1780. SHEFFIELD's State of Ireland.

of

of trade, and to diſtribute its bounties and protections in ſuch an equal manner among all
claſſes of manufactures, that they may have no
private or detached intereſt, but growing up
together in due ſubordination, may form one
compact ſyſtem of national induſtry.

F I N I S.